The William and Marion Haas Research Fund

NORTHWESTERN UNIVERSITY

Studies in Geography

Number 12

THE INTERNAL STRUCTURE OF RETAIL NUCLEATIONS

Barry J. Garner

Department of Geography
Northwestern University
Evanston, Illinois
1966

For

Ada and Bill

84787

ACKNOWLEDGMENTS

Many of the ideas contained in this work were crystalized during the writer's period of graduate study at Northwestern University under the supervision of Professor E. J. Taaffe, now of the Department of Geography, The Ohio State University. I would like to express my sincere thanks to Professor Taaffe for the many hours of stimulating guidance and encouragement which culminated in the completion of the doctoral dissertation from which this work is taken. I also owe a special debt of gratitude to Professor B. J. L. Berry of the University of Chicago for his active interest in discussing and criticizing the ideas presented here, and for giving me the opportunity of working with the Commercial Study of the Community Renewal Program, City of Chicago, without which the original study could not have been undertaken. Sincere thanks are also extended to Bob Tennant and Sam Cullers for their help in gathering the data and for permission to reproduce it in Chapters II and III, and for all the help and encouragement given by members of the faculty and staff of the Department of Geography at Northwestern University that have made publication possible.

This volume is complementary to several others already published in the Research Paper Series, Department of Geography, University of Chicago. These are Brian J. L. Berry et al., Commercial Structure and Commercial Blight, Brian J. L. Berry and Robert J. Tennant, Chicago Commercial Reference Handbook, and James W. Simmons, The Changing Patterns of Retail Location.

Bristol, England
August, 1965

iii

TABLE OF CONTENTS

Page

ACKNOWLEDGMENTS   iii

LIST OF TABLES   vii

LIST OF ILLUSTRATIONS   xi

INTRODUCTION   xv

Chapter
   I. THE COMMERCIAL STRUCTURE AND LAND
       VALUE PATTERN OF THE CITY   1

  II. THE HIERARCHY OF RETAIL NUCLEATIONS   25

 III. THE FUNCTIONAL STRUCTURE OF RETAIL
       NUCLEATIONS   59

  IV. THE INTERNAL STRUCTURE OF RETAIL
       NUCLEATIONS   97

   V. THE RELATIONSHIP BETWEEN LAND VALUE
       AND LAND USE WITHIN RETAIL NUCLEATIONS   125

CONCLUSION   183

APPENDIX A - THE RELATIONSHIP BETWEEN COOK
             COUNTY ASSESSED VALUES AND
             OLCOTT'S "BLUE BOOK" VALUES IN
             THE CITY OF CHICAGO   185

APPENDIX B - THE DELIMITATION OF RETAIL
             NUCLEATIONS   189

APPENDIX C - TYPES OF RETAIL AND SERVICE
             BUSINESS   193

TABLE OF CONTENTS--Continued

Page

APPENDIX D - TESTING THE VALIDITY OF USING
A RANKING OF FUNCTIONS BY THEIR
FREQUENCY OF OCCURRENCE AT
CENTERS IN THE STUDY AREA AS A
VIABLE APPROXIMATION OF A RANKING
OF FUNCTIONS BY THRESHOLD SIZE   197

BIBLIOGRAPHY   205

LIST OF TABLES

Table	Page
1. The Commercial Structure of a City.	5
2. A Representative Sample of Functions Typical of Outlying Retail Nucleations	7
3. The Supply of "n" Goods from Four Levels of Retail Nucleations	15
4. The Retail Nucleations Included in the Study Area	28
5. Selected Size Relationships	33
6. Covariance Analysis on Elevations of Sub-Regression Lines	43
7. Covariance Analysis on Elevations of Sub-Regression Lines for Centers in the Rest of the City	43
8. Variance Analysis between the Log. Occupied Establishments and Number of Business Types for Centers in the Workingmen's Area	48
9. Variance Analysis between the Mean Floor Area Size of the Five Groups of Retail Nucleations	48
10. The Hierarchy of Retail Nucleations in the City of Chicago	52
11. Summary of the Fundamental Characteristics of the Hierarchy of Retail Nucleations in the City of Chicago, 1961	56
12. Central Functions	61
13. Addresses and Peak Values of Sample Nucleations	64
14. Neighborhood Level Functions	67
15. The Functional Structure of Neighborhood Level Sample Centers	69

LIST OF TABLES--Continued

Table   Page

16. Percentage Composition of Level of Center by S.I.C. Groups 70

17. Community Level Functions 71

18. The Functional Structure of Community Level Sample Centers . . . . 74 & 75

19. Regional Level Functions 76

20. The Functional Structure of Regional Level Sample Centers . . . . 78 & 79

21. The Functional Structure of Workingmen's Minor Sample Centers . . . . 80 & 81

22. The Functional Structure of Workingmen's Major Sample Centers . . . . 82 & 83

23. Peak Value Data by Level of Center 92

24. Variance Analysis between Mean Peak Values and Level of Center 92

25. Difference in Mean Peak Land Value between Individual Levels in the Hierarchy of Retail Nucleations 93

26. Central Functions Ranked by Frequency of Occurrence at Retail Nucleations in the City of Chicago 128

27. Mean Percent Land Values for Functions by Level of Center 130

28. Clustering of Neighborhood Level Functions 136

29. Clustering of Community Level Functions 138

30. Clustering of Regional Level Functions 140

31. Functions with Large Rank Differences 142

LIST OF TABLES--Continued

Table   Page

32. Significant Rank Correlations between Land Value and
    Threshold Size   145

33. The Internal Structure of Neighborhood Centers by
    S. I. C. Groups   147

34. The Internal Structure of Neighborhood Centers   148

35. The Internal Structure of Community Centers
    by S. I. C. Groups   149

36. The Internal Structure of Community Centers   150

37. The Internal Structure of Regional Centers
    by S. I. C. Groups   152

38. The Internal Structure of Regional Centers . . . . . 154 & 155

39. The Internal Structure of Minor Centers
    by S. I. C. Groups   158

40. The Internal Structure of Major Centers
    by S. I. C. Groups   158

41. The Internal Structure of Minor Centers   160

42. The Internal Structure of Major Centers   161

43. Variability in Land Values by Function . . . . 178 & 179

44. Relationships between Olcott's and Assessed
    Land Values   185

45. The Ranking of Functions by Number of Establishments
    in the Chicago S. M. A. and Frequency of Occurrence
    at Centers in the Study Area   197

46. Ranking of Select Functions in Snohomish County
    (Washington), Grant County (Wisconsin), and the
    Chicago Study Area   198

LIST OF ILLUSTRATIONS

Figure   Page

1. Regression of Log. Occupied Establishments on Number of Business Types 34

2. Regression of Log. Floor Area on Number of Business Types 35

3. Retail Nucleations with more Occupied Establishments and Larger Floor Area than Expected 38

4. Sub-Regression of Log. Occupied Establishments on Number of Business Types 40

5. Sub-Regression of Log. Floor Area on Number of Business Types 41

6. Sub-Regression of Log. Establishments on Number of Business Types for Different Levels of Center in the Rest of the City 45

7. The Relationship between Occupied Establishments and Number of Business Types in Centers in the Workingmen's Area 46

8. The Hierarchy of Retail Nucleations in the City of Chicago, 1961 51

9. An Idealized K=4 System of Retail Nucleations in the City of Chicago 55

10. The Distribution of Sample Nucleations 63

11. Diagrammatic Representation of the Shift in Functional Structure of the Workingmen's Centers 86

12. The Proportion of Total Floor Area Devoted to Convenience, Shopping and Other Goods by Level of Retail Nucleation 88

Figure   Page

13. Selected Relationships between Functional Structure
    and Physical Characteristics in the Hierarchy of
    Retail Nucleations   91

14. The Relationship between Peak Value and Number of
    Business Types by Level of Retail Nucleation   95

15. Ideal Relationship between Sales and Distance at a
    Regional Center   106

16. Ideal Relationship between Sales and Distance at
    Different Levels in an Hierarchy   106

17. The Relationship between Rents and Threshold Sales   108

18. Hypothetical Rent Gradients for Two Business Types   108

19. Hypothetical Rent Gradients for Typical Regional,
    Community and Neighborhood Level Business Types   110

20. Hypothetical Internal Structure of Regional,
    Community and Neighborhood Level Retail Nucleations   112

21. The Threshold Continuum   119

22. Hypothetical Rent Gradients for Product Differentiated
    Business Types   122

23. Hypothetical Internal Structure of a Regional Center
    when Product Differentiation Exists   124

24. Range in Land Values of Neighborhood Functions . . .   167

25. Range in Land Values of Functions in Community
    Level Nucleations   168

26. Range in Land Values of Functions in Regional Level
    Nucleations   169

27. Range in Land Values of Functions in Minor Centers   174

LIST OF ILLUSTRATIONS--Continued

Figure   Page

28. Range in Land Values of Functions in
    Major Centers 175

29. Land Value Profiles at 63rd and Cottage Grove 188

INTRODUCTION

The purpose of this study is twofold: (1) to identify a hierarchy of nucleated outlying business centers in the City of Chicago in 1961, and (2) to describe, and as far as is possible, to explain patterns in the ground floor arrangement of functions within business centers at different levels in the hierarchy. The analysis of internal structure is based on the relationship between land values and commercial land use, and the entire work is set in the framework of the theory of tertiary activity.

The major findings are as follows:

(1) There is more than one hierarchy of nucleated outlying business centers within the City of Chicago. Different hierarchies are related to spatial differences in socio-economic characteristics of the city's neighborhoods.

(2) The underlying premises of the theory of tertiary activity and the theory of land values are interrelated in such a way as to result in a logical ordering of functions within business centers. Order in arrangement is founded upon the premise that high threshold functions are at the same time high rent paying functions. The functions which set a center above others in the hierarchy show a tendency to occupy its high value core and are surrounded concentrically on lower value land by the functions characteristic of each preceding level of center.

(3) The underlying order of the internal structure of business centers becomes more complex within high order centers on account of distortions introduced by product differentiation and the locational effects of buying habits and space consumption.

(4) Certain functions are not located within nucleations according to their threshold size. This is especially true of the higher order space-consuming functions such as furniture stores, which tend to concentrate on low value land toward the periphery of regional centers, and of drug stores, candy stores, and the lower order clothing functions, which maintain their central locations within nucleations despite changes of level.

(5) The threshold concept can be extended to include product differentiation when the thresholds used in current literature are viewed as the mean of a range of threshold sizes for each business type, and the threshold is competitive when equated to the possibilities of achieving scale economies.

Recent studies of the commercial structure of urban areas have shown that central place theory, when reformulated as a more general theory of tertiary activity, enables a logical description and explanation of a hierarchy of nucleated business centers within cities. However, to date, the theory has been used essentially as an allocational rather than a locational theory.

Central functions are allocated to business centers at the alternate levels in the hierarchy according to threshold size, but are not located at specific sites within them. By way of analogy, imagine a series of varying sized boxes, each corresponding to a center at a given level in the hierarchy, and a pack of cards, with each card representing a particular threshold function. The theory of tertiary activity enables the cards to be allocated to the different boxes according to their threshold sizes. But it does no more than this. The cards are not sorted inside the boxes; they lie in a jumbled heap. We identify the functional structure of a center but only deal with it in aggregate. Consequently, the theory of tertiary activity is not locational in the sense of assigning individual functions to specific locations within centers of any given level.

It is natural to use the theory of tertiary activity as a framework for the study, since the investigation deals only with the nucleated aspect of the urban commercial structure. Moreover, it is emphasized heavily because we feel that the premises upon which the theory is founded are also applicable in the study of intra-center locational patterns. Therefore, the theory can be more widely used to study the urban business complex than is currently fashionable.

The theory of tertiary activity permits statements to be made about the location of business activities within retail nucleations when it is related to the theory of land values. Since the utility of a given site within business centers can be measured by its rent, the greater the site utility for a particular function, the greater the rent it is willing to pay to use that site. By relating threshold sizes to site utility, alias rent-paying ability, the two theories can be wedded to generate models of the idealized internal structure of retail nucleations. Such models form the basis of the investigation undertaken here.

Methods used in this work vary from the completely subjective to the more refined statistical procedures. Wherever possible, the method that best fits the problem has been used, although in some cases better methods could have been utilized had computing facilities been available at the time of analysis. This is especially true, for example, of taxonomic problems in the study. In this respect, heavy reliance is placed on the findings of other researchers. However, the generalizations have been formulated as objectively as possible and can therefore be considered as a meaningful and valid approximation of the real world.

The work is essentially divided into two parts: the first three chapters are concerned with the identification of a hierarchy of retail nucleations within the City of Chicago; the remainder of the work is devoted to the analysis of the internal structure of centers at various levels in the hierarchy.

In Chapter I, background material about the urban business pattern is presented. A brief discussion of the early writings is complemented by the introduction of some ideas from central place theory, notions of accessibility and retail location, and the important notions concerning the relationships between land values and the commercial pattern. Chapters II and III deal with the delimitation of a hierarchy of retail nucleations within the City of Chicago, 1961 and the functional structure of centers at different levels within the hierarchy.

The internal structure of retail nucleations is dealt with in Chapters IV and V. In the former, a simple model is developed to explain the arrangement of functions within nucleations, and more complex systems are proposed in order to take into account product differentiation. These are based upon the relaxation of the rigid operational definition of the threshold. The last chapter is devoted to the testing of the models. The work is concluded with a short section on topics considered important for future study.

CHAPTER I

THE COMMERCIAL STRUCTURE AND LAND VALUE
PATTERN OF THE CITY

During the past twenty-five years, innumerable books and articles
have been written about various aspects of retailing activity in urban
areas. The important contributions to this literature have been
summarized elsewhere, [1] and the few findings pertinent to an understanding of spatial structure were recently incorporated into a more
exhaustive study of the geography of urban retail activity. [2] Hence,
we need only provide a brief review here.

---

[1] A complete discussion of the early literature is to be found in
Helen G. Canoyer, "Selecting a Store Location", Economic Series
No. 56, (Washington, D.C.: Office of Domestic Commerce, United
States Department of Commerce, 1946). Also see B. J. L. Berry
and A. Pred, Central Place Studies -- A Bibliography of Theory and
Applications, (Regional Science Research Institute, Bibliography
Series No. 1; Philadelphia, 1961), especially section XXVI, pp. 63-
72.

[2] B. J. L. Berry, "Shopping Centers in the Geography of Urban
Areas," (unpublished Ph.D. dissertation, University of Washington,
Seattle, 1958).

Among the early descriptions of the commercial structure of the
city, the works of Rolph,[3] Proudfoot,[4] and Ratcliff[5] are perhaps the
most important, providing good examples of the level of investigation
in the pioneer literature. The underlying theme of these works is the
sub-classification of the three basic components in the retail pattern,
namely, the C. B. D., the outlying nucleation, and the "string street"
or ribbon development. In the post-war period, Kelley provided a
similar description of the commercial structure of the city based on
the generally accepted distinctions between planned and unplanned
neighborhood, community, and regional shopping centers.[6]

However, these early writings greatly oversimplified the pattern
of commercial activity. This was due, in part, to the high level of

[3] I. K. Rolph, "The Locational Structure of Retail Trade,"
Domestic Commerce Series, No. 80, (Washington, D. C.: United
States Bureau of Commerce, Domestic and Foreign, 1929); also
idem, "Nucleation: The Pattern of Retail Marketing," in The Metro-
politan Community, ed. R. D. McKenzie, (New York: McGraw Hill
Book Co., 1933), pp. 250-266.

[4] M. J. Proudfoot, Intra City Business Census Statistics for
Philadelphia, (Washington, D.C.: United States Department of
Commerce, 1937); idem, "City Retail Structure," Economic
Geography, XIII (1937), pp. 425-428. For a more complete description
of the major outlying nucleations, see idem "The Major Outlying
Business Centers of Chicago," (unpublished Ph. D. dissertation,
University of Chicago, 1936).

[5] R. U. Ratcliff, Urban Land Economics, (New York: McGraw
Hill Book Co., 1949). The arguments presented are developed more
fully in idem, "An examination into 'Some Characteristics of
Outlying Retail Nucleations in the City of Detroit,'" (unpublished Ph. D.
dissertation, University of Michigan, 1935), and idem, "The Problem
of Retail Site Selection," Michigan Business Studies, IX (1939), 1-33.

[6] E. J. Kelley, Shopping Centers, (Saugatuck, Conn.: Eno
Foundation for Highway Traffic Control, 1956), pp. 66-67.

data aggregation (with, perhaps, Kelley's work excepted), in part to the lack of a sound theoretical framework for analysis, and in part to the emphasis upon form rather than function. As a result, rather simple, descriptive statements of morphological diversity were adopted in preference to an understanding of the basic processes involved in the generation of the retail pattern. It is not surprising, therefore, that neither a clear understanding of a hierarchy of retail nucleations based upon function was realized, nor that many differences in the locational requirements of retail functions are at the basis of the variety of components of that pattern. Moreover, no consideration was given to the arrangement of functions within any of the described components.

The listing of types, generation of broad classifications, and the presentation of limited, supporting empirical evidence was by itself inadequate. What was needed was a process-oriented theoretical framework of analysis for the development of more meaningful generalizations, and a more viable description of the urban business pattern.

This need was satisfied by Berry who derived a more complete description of the urban business pattern by combining earlier findings with the results of, (a) theoretically guided empirical studies of Spokane; (b) comparative analysis of Phoenix and Cincinnati; (c) a sample of planned shopping centers across the United States; and (d) a study of developments along Seattle-Everett U. S. 99.[7] Additional insight into the nature of urban business structure is gained from more recent studies of a portion of the Chicago metropolitan area by the

[7]B. J. L. Berry, "Shopping Centers....., " op. cit.

same writer.[8] Extensive field observation by this author in the City
of Chicago confirms the viability of Berry's taxonomy.

The retail and service structure of the metropolitan area can best
be described as a complex. Outside the C. B. D. , it is possible to
differentiate between three major conformations and a variety of
isolated or "freestanding" business types. These conformations are:
(a) the nucleated center; (b) the ribbon development; and (c) the
specialized district. The complete sub-classification of these types
is shown in Table I. Identification of these groups is from an analysis
of the locational characteristics of all commercial functions, and not
merely from a consideration of morphological differences which
typified the earlier writings. Consequently, the functional structure
of each component is specified. Moreover, since the system is based
in part upon a process-oriented theoretical base, a greater understanding of the rationale of such systems is available. In this work
we are concerned only with nucleations or outlying business centers.

The Hierarchy of Retail Nucleations

Retail nucleations in the urban area consist of clusters of retail
activities at important street intersections. They usually constitute
foci at the intersection of two or more ribbon developments, where
high vehicular and pedestrian traffic intensity provides the focus for
growth. On primary streets they may arise at intervals within ribbon
developments whilst in some cases, especially with smaller nucleations,
they may string out as local shopping streets.

[8] B. J. L. Berry and H. M. Mayer, Comparative Studies of
Central Place Systems, (United States Navy, Office of Naval Research,
Project NONR 2121 - 18; NR 389 - 126), Department of Geography,
University of Chicago, 1962.

5

TABLE 1

THE COMMERCIAL STRUCTURE OF A CITY

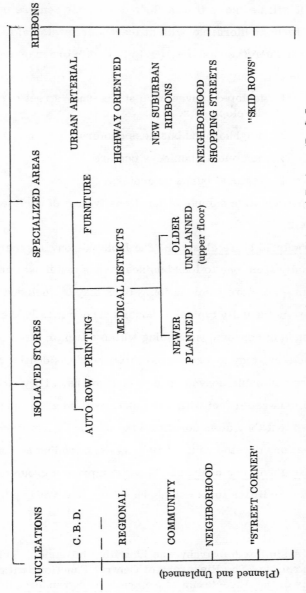

Source: B. J. L. Berry, The Commercial Structure of American Cities -- A Review. (Draft Copy, Community Renewal Program, City of Chicago, February 1962.)

It will be shown that nucleated business centers in the metropolitan area form an hierarchy with at least four levels below that of the Central Business District, (C. B. D.).[9] In order of ascending functional complexity, they are:

1. isolated convenience stores and "street corner" developments.

2. neighborhood business centers.

3. community business centers.

4. regional business centers.

A representative sample of functions typical of each level is shown in Table 2.

Isolated store clusters. The isolated convenience group comprises normally from one to four business types and most commonly is the grocer-drugstore combination. Bars may be included at this level, but are not usually typical. Serving predominantly the occasional demands of consumers residing within a two or three block radius of the cluster, they are scattered throughout residential neighborhoods to ensure maximum convenience to consumers. They constitute the most ubiquitous retail foci within the metropolitan area, and it has been argued that they often constitute the original germ from which larger nucleations develop as the city grows and trading areas mature.[10]

Neighborhood centers. These comprise a group of retail and service facilities for a neighborhood to allow ready purchase of major

[9]A similar hierarchy was identified in Zurich, Switzerland, by H. Carol, in "The Hierarchy of Central Functions within the City," Annals of the Association of American Geographers, 50 (1960), pp. 419-438.

[10]R. U. Ratcliff, "The Problem of Retail Site Selection," op. cit.

TABLE 2

A REPRESENTATIVE SAMPLE
OF FUNCTIONS TYPICAL OF OUTLYING RETAIL NUCLEATIONS

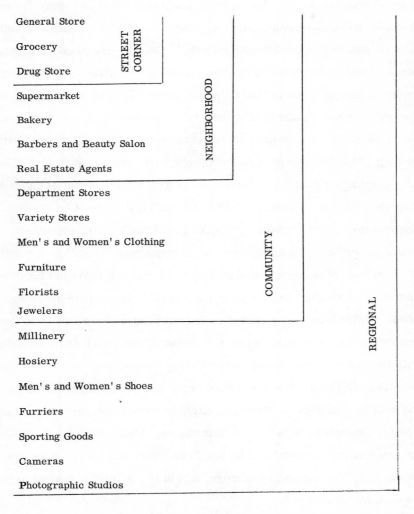

General Store

Grocery

Drug Store

Supermarket

Bakery

Barbers and Beauty Salon

Real Estate Agents

Department Stores

Variety Stores

Men's and Women's Clothing

Furniture

Florists

Jewelers

Millinery

Hosiery

Men's and Women's Shoes

Furriers

Sporting Goods

Cameras

Photographic Studios

STREET CORNER

NEIGHBORHOOD

COMMUNITY

REGIONAL

Source: B. J. L. Berry, "Ribbon Developments in the Urban Business
          Pattern," Annals of the Association of American Geographers,
          Vol. 49, (1959), 147.

necessities from locations of immediate convenience to the consumer. They include the grocery and small supermarkets, drugstore, laundries and dry cleaners, barber and/or beauty salons, and cheap eating and drinking places. Occasionally real estate, insurance offices and hardware stores are found. Ratcliff has found that these are more frequently found in areas undergoing socio-economic change, or areas characterized by substantial residential growth.[11] Neighborhood centers serve home-based convenience trips for consumers residing in the immediate vicinity, but embrace larger tributary areas than are served from the "street corner" clusters. Furthermore, neighborhood centers service the trade areas of a number of "street corner" clusters, resulting in nesting of the latter within the former's trade area.

Community centers. These exhibit greater functional complexity than the lower level centers, and mark the beginnings of true retail nucleations. They contain a group of retail and service facilities provided for the community (several neighborhoods) to allow for both the purchase of necessities associated with the neighborhood function and less specialized and frequently demanded comparison shopping goods. In addition, they provide entertainment and a group of business and office services required by a community and which are compatible with the other uses. Variety and clothing stores, dairies, confectioners, jewelers, florists and a post office are added to the functions present at the neighborhood level. Service activities include lawyers, insurance agents, real estate agents and, sometimes, branch banks. Since branch banking is prohibited by law in the State of Illinois, they are replaced by the currency exchange, which is considered typical at this level in the study area.

[11]R. U. Ratcliff, "An Examination into Some Characteristics...," op. cit., Chapter III.

Regional centers. The highest order of the outlying retail nucleations provides goods and services for a region comprising several community areas, to allow for the purchase of all, except the most specialized commodities which are presumed to be offered in the C.B.D. They are set above community centers not so much by the types of functions as in the number and variety offered. Department stores, specialized furniture stores, specialized clothing stores, music and record stores, and other more specialized business types are added to the functions typical of lower level nucleations. Banks and a wide range of personal, professional and business services are typical. Although regional centers serve home-based trips in the same way as the lower level nucleations, they allow for greater variety of consumer purchases, and thus greater multiplicity of shopping trip purpose. Regional centers are, as a result, the foci of much larger trading areas often totaling many square miles depending upon the density of population and availability of purchasing power.

Above the lowest level in the hierarchy, the more recently developed business centers may be planned, especially in the newer areas of the city. The rationale for distinguishing between planned and unplanned nucleations is immediately obvious. However, such distinction is based solely on the difference between controlled development on the one hand and natural evolution on the other. Functionally, there is no difference between the two types, although morphologically and in number of establishments, they may in fact vary considerably.

The Theory of Tertiary Activity and Retail Nucleations

The existence of an hierarchy of centers within the urban business complex can be explained by the premises of central place theory,[12]

---

[12]W. Christaller, Die zentralen Orte in Suddeutschland (Jena: Gustav Fischer, 1933), translated by C. Baskin, "Central Place Theory,"

modified as a more general theory of tertiary activity to embrace the urban scene. The ideas of the range of a good and the threshold are particularly important. Berry describes the range of a good as follows:

> "This range marks out the zone or tributary area around a central place (retail nucleation), from which persons travel to the center to purchase the good, '..... a product of the simultaneous effects of all the factors of demand and supply involved in the purchase of central goods and services', (Christaller, 1937, p. 20). The upper limit of the range is the maximum possible radius of sales. Beyond the upper limit the price of the good is too high for it to be sold either because of the increase in price with distance until consumers will no longer purchase the good (the ideal limit where demand becomes zero), or because of the greater proximity of consumers to an alternate competing center (the real limit). The range also has a lower limit, that radius which encloses the minimum numbers of consumers necessary to provide a sales volume adequate for the good to be supplied profitably from the central place." [13]

The range of a good thus defines the market area of a business center for a specific business type.

The minimum sales level enclosed by the lower limit is called the threshold. This is the point at which sales are just large enough for the firm to cover costs of operation and earn normal profits. When

---

(unpublished Ph. D. dissertation, University of Virginia, 1955).

A. Lösch, Die raümliche Ordung der Wirtschaft, (Jena: Gustav Fischer, second edition, 1943), translated by H. Woglom and W. F. Stolper as The Economics of Location, (New Haven, Conn.: Yale University Press, 1954).

[13] B. J. L. Berry and W. L. Garrison, "A Note on Central Place Theory and the Range of a Good," Economic Geography, 34 (1958), pp. 304-311.

the threshold is not satisfied, there is no economic justification for the good to be provided from a business center. The threshold therefore represents a minimal size of market, or condition of entry, defined by the lower limit to the range of a business type from a center. All business types do not require the same level of sales to earn normal profit.[14] In fact, each type is ordered depending upon the size of its threshold, such that

$$S_1 < S_2 < S_3 < \ldots < S_m \qquad (1:1)$$

where S_m is the threshold of the highest order business type.

From the array (1:1), the number of business types and the number of establishments of each type in the urban area is determined for any value S_m. Assuming that when there are enough sales to satisfy the threshold of type $\underline{m}$, and all lower threshold business types are provided, it follows that the number of types is a function of the threshold population or sales level of type $\underline{m}$, and since types are ordered from i = 1 to $\underline{m}$, the number of business types does in fact equal $\underline{m}$.

$$\sum_{i=1}^{m} T_i = \underline{m} \qquad (i = 1 \text{ to } \underline{m}) \qquad (1:2)$$

where T_i is business type $\underline{i}$. For example, if the total threshold population or sales level is just large enough to support the third highest threshold type ($\underline{m} = 3$), and all lower level types are represented, then three business types would be present.

Further, if sales or threshold population in the urban area is an

---

[14]The following definitions are used: (a) Business Type: a type of activity, such as drug stores or women's clothing stores, as listed in the Standard Industrial Classification: (b) Establishments: a store performing one or more business types.

exact multiple of the threshold of each type, the number of establishments of each individual type in the urban area is:

$$E_i = f(S_m) \tag{1:3}$$

where E_i is the number of establishments of business type $\underline{i}$. For
example, imagine the total population or sales level is just large enough
to support the third highest type ($\underline{m} = 3$), and that $S_m = 10$ units. If
the thresholds S_1 and S_2 are two units and five units respectively, then
five establishments of type 1, two establishments of type 2 and one
establishment of type 3 will be represented.

From this it follows that there is an ordering of types by the
number of establishments, since the number of establishments of each
business type decreases with increasing thresholds.

$$E_1 > E_2 > E_3 > \ldots \ldots > E_m \tag{1:4}$$

Consequently, the lowest threshold type will be the most ubiquitous in
the urban area, and each succeeding type will be characterized by
decreasing ubiquity of occurrence. It is important to remember this
fact.

The total number of establishments in the urban area is a function
of the threshold of the highest business type represented.

$$\sum_{i=1}^{m} E_i = g(m) \quad (i = 1 \text{ to } m) \tag{1:5}$$

Thus, for example, when $\underline{m} = 3$, and $S_m = 10$ and given that $S_1 = 2$
and $S_2 = 5$, a total of eight establishments will be represented,
comprising five of type 1, two of type 2 and one of type 3 respectively.

When the total threshold population or sales level is large enough
to support more than one establishment of type $\underline{m}$ ($E_m > 1$), but not
large enough to support type S_{m+1}, (1:3) can also be written

$$E_i = f(E_m) \tag{1:6}$$

and the total number of establishments of all types can be obtained by summing over all E_i. For example, if the total threshold population is 20 units, $S_m = 10$ (when $\underline{m} = 3$) and $S_{m+1} = 21$, there would be insufficient thresholds for S_{m+1} to appear, but two establishments of S_3 could exist in the urban area. Given thresholds $S_1 = 2$ and $S_2 = 5$ as above, then the total number of establishments of types 1, 2 and 3, would be ten, four and two respectively. Summing establishments over all types would give a total of sixteen establishments in the urban area.

Retail stores are indivisible. Thus it is impossible to have a fraction of a store. Consequently, any sales in the urban area that are in excess of an exact multiple of threshold for any S_i, but not large enough to justify the appearance of another establishment of that type, will be provided for by the existing number of establishments (E_i). With the possibility for excess demand over supply at threshold to exist in this way, profits in excess of the "normal" may be earned and ranges will reach a more competitive upper limit. From this, relationships (1:3) and (1:6) hold and imply variation in the size of establishments above threshold level.

Moreover, given the existence of hierarchical marginal goods in array (1:1), extension of the arguments presented above demonstrate that equations (1:1) through (1:6) hold also with respect to the number of business types and establishments at any level of retail nucleation within the urban area.[15]

---

[15] The notion of the hierarchical good was developed by B. J. L. Berry, who provides the following definition: "But there may be one or more goods, say good n - i, in which case the interstitial purchasing power located between threshold market areas of $\underline{A}$ centers supplying good n - i will reach threshold size. . . good n - i may be termed a hierarchical good." See B. J. L. Berry, "Shopping Centers . . . ," op. cit. p. 32.

For example, assume business type m - j is a hierarchical marginal good. S_{m-j} will be the highest threshold satisfied from that level retail nucleation. The number of business types at that center will be given.

$$\sum_{i=1}^{m-j} T_i = m-j \qquad (1:8)$$

and the total number of establishments in the nucleation is given

$$\sum_{i=1}^{m-j} E_i = f(E_{m-j}) \qquad (1:9)$$

Thus if S_{m-k}, S_{m-1} are thresholds of hierarchical marginal goods for community and neighborhood level centers respectively, the above relationships hold for each lower level retail nucleation in the hierarchy. An example of the distribution of activities between alternate level centers resulting from this is shown in Table 3. All retail nucleations (business centers) in the system are assumed to be located at the most efficient least cost point of supply central to maximum profit areas at their command. Under this assumption, normal profit levels will be reached, excess profits will be evenly distributed, and the notion of accessibility is defined.

The characteristic elements of the hierarchy can now be generalized as follows:

1. Low level nucleations offer only low level goods and serve tributary areas defined by the lower range hierarchical marginal good. Low level goods are generally necessities requiring frequent purchase, and correspond to the "convenience" goods in the planning literature. Low level nucleations will be the most ubiquitous in the system.

2. Higher level nucleations provide not only higher threshold goods, but all lower types also. Higher threshold goods correspond to the "shopping" goods identified in the planning literature, and for which consumers are prepared to travel longer distances although less

TABLE 3

THE SUPPLY OF "n" GOODS FROM FOUR LEVELS OF RETAIL NUCLEATIONS

LEVEL OF NUCLEATION	GOODS			
	m*, m – 1, ...	m–j*, m–(j+1), ...	m–k*, m–(k+1), ...	m–l*, m–(l+1), ...1
C.B.D.	X	X	X	⋮ X
Regional		X	X	⋮ X
Community			X	⋮ X
Neighborhood				X

Notes: * indicates a hierarchical marginal good
      X indicates the set of goods supplied from the nucleation

Source: B. J. L. Berry, "Shopping Centers in the Geography of Urban Areas," Unpublished Ph. D. dissertation, Department of Geography, University of Washington, Seattle, 1958, p. 33.

frequently. Higher level nucleations will be less ubiquitous than lower level nucleations.

3. Nucleations at any level will offer more goods, have more establishments, more business types, serve larger tributary areas and tributary populations, and have higher total sales volumes than any nucleation below that level.

4. Since the above relationship exists, a complex pattern of nested trade areas results and any consumer is served most efficiently by the closest and most accessible nucleation of any higher level.[16]

Factors Affecting the Location of Retail Nucleations

Outlying business centers are not uniformly distributed within the urban area. Real world patterns are conditioned by intra-urban differences in accessibility and by the markedly uneven distribution of population densities, disposable incomes and tastes. Distortion from expected patterns can also be the result of zoning ordinances.[17]

The quality of location, or accessibility, is the dominant factor in determining the uses of land and its intensity of development. Wingo states that, "In a technical sense, accessibility is a relative quality accruing to a parcel of land by virtue of its relationship to a transporta tion system operating at some specific level of service".[18] The basic

---

[16] A succinct description of the basic elements of the hierarchy is found in B. J. L. Berry and A. Pred, Central Place Studies, op. cit., pp. 3-14.

[17] For a discussion of the effects of zoning on the distortion of theoretically sound distributions, see A. Getis, "The Determination of the Location of Retail Activities with the use of Map Transformations," Economic Geography, XXXIX (1963), 14-22.

[18] L. Wingo, Transportation and Urban Land, (Washington D. C.: Resources for the Future, Inc., 1961), p. 26.

importance of accessibility in the generation of the hierarchy of retail
nucleations has already been stressed above. Each business center is
assumed to be located at the least-cost point central to the maximum
profit area at its command.

But buyers and sellers are scattered over wide areas within the
city, and movement between them is impeded. Differences in degrees
of accessibility are primarily conditioned by the existing pattern of
transportation routes. Accessibility is highest along high-speed routes
and especially where two or more such routes intersect. Mention is
made above of the tendency for retail nucleations to form at such intersections.

Each level in the hierarchy of retail nucleations is located at sites
most accessible to the portion of the urban market it serves.
Presumably then, higher level centers with greater numbers of
establishments and business types are associated with higher degrees
of accessibility than lower level centers. From this, the following
relationship holds

$$\sum_{i=1}^{m} T_i = f(X) \qquad (1:10)$$

where X is accessibility within the urban area. Similarly, since from
(1: 5) above, then

$$\sum_{i=1}^{m} E_i = g(X) \qquad (1:11)$$

where $\sum_{i=1}^{m} E_i$ is the total number of establishments at any level
nucleation.

Accessibility, as used above, reflects lines of least resistance in
overcoming the frictions of distance separating buyer from seller.
Hence, the spatial pattern assumed by the hierarchy obviously relates
to the pattern of movement and traffic flow within a city. Here it can
be measured by the variations in friction of distance inherent in the

rectangular grid street pattern, and as a result, the spatial distribution of the hierarchy is affected by variation in accessibility afforded by the basic gridded street pattern in urban areas.

Added deviation from the theoretically uniform distribution of retail nucleations within the urban areas can be accounted for by the complexities of the urban market outlined above. The spatial distribution of retail centers is conditioned critically by the spatial distribution of disposable income. Where this is available in large amounts due to the concentration of consumers within small areas, centers of each level will be closely spaced. Similarly, where the converse is true, then centers will be spaced further apart.

Besides the effect that the nature of the urban market has upon the spacing of centers, the nature of the demand influences the types of goods offered from centers. On the one hand, the urban market consists of people with widely different amounts of disposable incomes; on the other, it consists of people with different ethnic and social backgrounds. Both of these features create a wide variation in the level of demand, and since this is related to variation in tastes, needs and preferences, it creates a wide variety of the kinds of goods demanded. Consequently, as the differences in the urban market become more and more marked, retail nucleations can vary locally with respect to the kinds of functions offered from them.[19] When these differences are characteristic of large areas in cities, such as for example the areas of depressed purchasing power associated with populations of lower-classes, the effect may be to create a local hierarchy of retail nucleations that is characterized by marked differences in types and numbers of businesses offered.

---

[19]For an example of this see A. Pred, "Business Thoroughfares as Expressions of Urban Negro Culture," Economic Geography, XXXIX (1963), 217-233.

Land Values and Retail Structure

The theory of urban land values is a curious mixture of broad generalizations concerning the future of urban land values, the application of classical rent theory to hypothetical isolated communities under certain assumed conditions and the classification of multiple demand and supply influences. Economists argue that it is the formation of people into communities that gives rise to the scarcity of urban land and hence its value.

The emphasis upon location as the basis of urban land values originates in the early writings of Ricardo and especially of von Thünen, who traced variations in agricultural land rents (and hence value) to differences in soil productivity and location in a theoretically isolated community.[20] Since the early work of von Thünen, many writers, and notably Haig[21] and Ratcliff,[22] stressed the importance of location, or relative accessibility, in the formation of land values in the urban area.

The Pattern of Land Values

Land values reach a peak in the central area of the city, and decline with increasing distance from that point. The decline in land values is not, however, characterized by a smooth curve. Rather, it comprises an irregular surface which declines in general away from the peak area, but which is broken by minor elevations or peakings.

[20] J. H. von Thünen, Der Isolierte Staat, (Jena: Gustav Fischer, 1842).

[21] R. M. Haig, "Toward an Understanding of the Metropolis," Quarterly Journal of Economics, 40 (1926), pp. 179-208 and 402-434; also idem, "Major Factors in Metropolitan Growth and Arrangement," in Regional Survey of New York and its Environs, (New York: Regional Plan of New York and its Environs, 1927), p. 39.

[22] R. U. Ratcliff, Urban Land Economics, op. cit.

More specifically, ridges of higher value radiate from the central peak along major traffic arteries, with the backs of each ridge gradually declining as a function of distance from the central major peak. Between each ridge there are plains, or plateaus, of varying elevation separated from each other by circumferential ridges running from radial to radial ridge. At the points of contact between radial and circumferential ridges, land value peaks of varying elevation occur.[23]

This somewhat simplified and romantic description of the land value pattern is rendered more complex, however, by the modifications imposed by the street pattern. Where this is essentially gridded in form, with few truly radial and circumferential arteries, the peaks occur at more regular intervals and are more evenly spaced in the system.

The plains and plateaus are by and large occupied by residential and industrial uses. Variation in the elevation of these surfaces results from a wide range of factors. In the case of residential areas, variations in socio-economic characteristics of the market for land are of prime importance; the nature of industrial development affects the levels of value in the industrial areas.[24] In contrast to these areas, variation in the level of ridges of value is related to corresponding variation in traffic intensity along the arteries. Similarly, variations in the level of the minor peaks in the land value surface are accounted for by differences in the relative accessibility of the street intersections at these points.

[23] For a vivid description of the land value surface for the City of Chicago, see H. Hoyt, One Hundred Years of Land Values in Chicago, (Chicago: University of Chicago Press, 1934).

[24] For an account of the factors influencing land values, and especially the importance attached to factors affecting the general level and those related to specific site variations, see P. Wendt, "A Theory of Urban Land Values," Land Economics, 33 (1957), pp. 228-240.

The Relationship to Retail Land Use

The pattern of ridges and minor peaking of land values corresponds
nicely to the pattern of commercial activity shown in Table 1. The
ridges are associated with the various types of ribbon development;
the level of land values and the intensity of retail development are
contingent upon the intensity of traffic along the arteries. The minor
peakings are associated with the retail nucleations comprising the
hierarchy. Early recognition of this association is contained in the
writings of Mayer and McKenzie, who both provide evidence of differ-
ential peaking of land values at major traffic intersections in association
with retail land uses.[25]

If differences in the elevation of land value peaks are assumed to
result from differences in accessibility at those points, it follows that

$$V_{pk} = h\ (X) \tag{1:12}$$

where V_{pk} represents the highest value at the intersection, the peak
value, and X accessibility. Thus, the greater the accessibility, the
higher the peak value, and thus the level of the minor land value
peaking.

From (1:10), however,

$$\sum_{i=1}^{m} T_i = f\,(X) \tag{1:10}$$

it follows that

$$V_{pk} = g\ (\sum_{i=1}^{m} T_i) \tag{1:13}$$

This yields an interesting feature in the relationship between the
retail structure and the pattern of land values because it implies that

---

[25] H. M. Mayer, "Patterns and Recent Trends in Chicago's
Outlying Business Centers," The Journal of Land and Public Utility
Economics, 18 (1942), pp. 4-16; and R. D. McKenzie, The Metropolitan
Community, op cit., pp. 236-238.

stratification of retail nucleations into levels of the hierarchy also implies stratification in general value levels, since both are associated with the same degree of accessibility. Therefore, land values may be used as an index of the relative importance of retail nucleations. This is of practical interest, since if (1:13) holds consistently, it should be possible to identify the hierarchy of retail nucleations in any city simply by comparing maps of land value and retail land use.

Dynamics of the System

The discussion so far has been based upon several assumptions, one of which has not specifically been brought to light. This is that the system is static and unchanging. In fact, this is clearly one of the major shortcomings of the theory of tertiary activity. Central places, whether they be hamlets, villages, and towns or neighborhood, community, and regional nucleations, do not pop up instantaneously in the landscape. They are not all the same age nor in the same stage of development. Rather, centers are at disparate stages of maturity; some are experiencing growth, others decline.[26]

The complex integrated urban landscape is especially dynamic, and constantly undergoing physical, economic, and social changes, which necessitate readjustment of all its parts to equilibrium positions. Characteristics of the urban market and accessibility patterns in the urban area are especially susceptible to such changes. Mobility to and within urban areas is reflected in invasion-succession cycles, and the subsequent modification of the nature of consumer demands.

[26]See R. L. Morrill, Migration and the Spread and Growth of Urban Settlement, (Lund, Sweden: Studies in Geography, Series B., Human Geography, No. 26, 1965); and J. S. Simmons, The Changing Pattern of Retail Location, (Chicago: University of Chicago, Department of Geography, Research Paper 92, 1964).

The transportation pattern is constantly modified by the addition of new and alternate routes, and modification of existing ones such that accessibility is variable through time. In turn, this is reflected in the pattern of land values which is also variable through time.[27]

Changes in the time dimension are most difficult to perceive when a cross-sectional analysis of these variables is undertaken. At any given moment in time, or in the growth cycle of retail nucleations, business centers should contain vestiges of former systems and incipient developments in anticipation of future ones. The former are probably more easily recognized than the latter.

Imagine a business center faced with declining demand -- either as a result of invasion-succession, or changed accessibility, or both. Under such a condition, it is reasonable to assume that threshold levels fall below the minimum required for certain business types. Evidence presented elsewhere indicates that when this happens the more specialized types drop out of the center first, followed by succeedingly lower threshold types, although subject to the willingness of small retailers to "hold on" in the short run by liquidation of capital.[28] Because of the "fixity of investment" in physical plant, an excess of store properties results. Vacancy rates should be high for awhile until either inferior goods enter under speculation, or non-retail uses take over the stores.

[27] R. U. Ratcliff, "The Dynamics of Efficiency in the Locational Distribution of Urban Activities," in The Metropolis and Modern Life, ed. R. Moore Fisher, (New York: Doubleday, 1955), pp. 125-148.

[28] R. H. Holton, "Price Discrimination at Retail: The Supermarket Case," Journal of Industrial Economics VI (1957) 13-32.

24

Accompanying decline, land values should also change, especially
if the underlying causation for decline in demand for land is to be
found in changing accessibility. The decline in land values is, however,
not instantaneous. Mayer mentions that, "land values do not immediately react to change in conditions affecting business area; there is
usually a lag of a year or two."[29]

[29]H. M. Mayer, "Patterns and Recent Trends......," op. cit., p. 8.

CHAPTER II

THE HIERARCHY OF RETAIL NUCLEATIONS

Hierarchies of central places have been most frequently identified from comparative analyses of the functional structure of service centers. A center is accorded an order in the hierarchy depending upon the number and types of goods and services offered to a surrounding and supporting tributary population.[1] In rural areas where such studies have been undertaken, for the most part attention has focused on functional composition for two reasons. Firstly, studies have only dealt with aggregates or total counts of all central functions present in varying sized, discrete settlements that stand apart from their rural surrounds. Secondly, it appears that central functions are distributed among centers at various levels in the hierarchy with a surprising step-like regularity.

---

[1] For an example of this approach, see B. J. L. Berry and W. L. Garrison, "Functional Bases of the Central Place Hierarchy," op. cit., and H. E. Bracey, "Towns as Rural Service Centers," Transactions and Papers, Institute of British Geographers, 19 (1953), pp. 95-105.

In metropolitan areas, however, where these conditions are less true, delimitation of a hierarchy is somewhat more difficult. In the first place, retail nucleations -- the counterpart of central places in rural areas -- cannot be so readily distinguished from other kinds of business conformations; and secondly, because of the high degree of mobility of urban populations and the resultant interdependence of all parts of the urban area, central functions are not distributed among the various business centers with anything like the regularity found in rural areas.

Identification and Delimitation of Centers

Given that retail nucleations are found in association with peakings of land value above the general level in any area, land value data is used for both the initial identification and subsequent delimitation of retail nucleations in the study area.

However, the use of land value data presents difficulties. For example, valuation data for a city may be established on either of two bases: appraisal or assessment. The main difficulty is determining which of these two sources represents most accurately the true market value of retail sites. Appraisal is intended to be a close approximation of the market value of the property, in contrast to assessment, which represents the legal valuation of property for tax purposes.[2] Both types of valuation data are available for the City of Chicago.

[2] For a more detailed account of these two evaluation schemes, see R. E. Murphy, J. E. Vance and B. L. Epstein, "Delimiting the C.B.D.," Economic Geography, XXX (1954), 197-200, and also B. J. Garner, "Land Values as a Method for Studying the Internal Structure of Central Business Districts", (mimeographed).

Appraised values are presented annually in Olcott's Blue Book, [3] and

are arrived at from the study of the sale of parcels of land in the urban

land market. Assessed values are available from the Cook County

Assessor's Office. From a study of the relationship between the two

sources of value data, the values presented in Olcott's Blue Book of

Chicago were used in this study. The results of this investigation are

presented in Appendix A.

In Chicago, most business land is valued at $150-$200 or more

per front foot and is located in association with ridges of higher land

value along traffic arteries. Where commercial development is

concentrated around major street intersections, values rise above the

level of the ridges to reach even higher peaks at the intersections

themselves. Moreover, it is readily apparent that the intensity of

development increases where peak values reach and are in excess of

$750 per front foot.

As an operational definition for this work, all places in the City

of Chicago which have land values higher than $750 per front foot in

association with commercial land use are considered as forming the

basis of a retail nucleation. Using this operational definition, Table 4

lists the sixty-two nucleations which were identified in the study area

with peak values ranging from $750 to $7,000 per front foot. Table 4

also lists a number of planned shopping centers in the city which were

used to illustrate some basic structural differences between planned

and unplanned retail nucleations in the analyses below.

[3] C. Olcott, Olcott's Land Value Blue Book of Chicago and
Suburbs, (Chicago: G. C. Olcott Co., 1961).

TABLE 4

THE RETAIL NUCLEATIONS INCLUDED IN THE STUDY AREA

Center	Peak Land Value ($ per front foot)	Center	Peak Land Value ($ per front foot)
63rd & Halsted	7000	North & Milwaukee	1200
Belmont & Ashland	5000	47th & South Parkway	1200
Madison & Pulaski	4000	Lawrence & Kedzie	1200
Irving Park & Cicero	4000	Lawrence & Western	1200
Diversey & Clark	2750	Howard & Paulina	1200
47th & Ashland	2500	79th & Ashland	1200
Lawrence & Broadway	2500	79th & Cottage Grove	1200
79th & Halsted	2500	26th & Pulaski	1100
111th & Michigan	2500	Devon & California	1000
Belmont & Central	2000	Bryn Mawr & Broadway	1000
Fullerton & Harlem	2000	Irving Park & Damen	1000
North & Pulaski	2000	63rd & Ashland	1000
Division & Clark	2000	67th & Stony Island	1000
Madison & Halsted	2000	Fullerton & Halsted	900
71st & Jeffrey	2000	63rd & Stony Island	900
91st & Commercial	1800	75th & Cottage	850
Lawrence & Milwaukee	1800	35th & Halsted	850
Diversey & Kimball	1750	Belmont & Cicero	850
Division & Ashland	1750	Madison & Ashland	800
63rd & Cottage Grove	1750	Lawrence & Damen	800
Roosevelt & Halsted	1700	Montrose & Broadway	800
Chicago & Ashland	1600	Irving Park & Sheridan	800
63rd & Western	1500	Madison & Western	800
53rd & Lake Park	1400	69th & Halsted	800
63rd & Kedzie	1400	Devon & Central	750
Devon & Western	1250	Roosevelt & Kedzie	750
North & California	1250	75th & Exchange	750
Madison & Central	1250	North & Larrabee	750
Madison & Cicero	1250	Fullerton & Cicero	750
Kinzie & Central	1200	Belmont & Clark	750
Madison & Kedzie	1200	63rd & Woodlawn	750

Planned Shopping Centers

Lake Meadows
Hyde Park (55th & Lake Park)
Chatham Park
95th & Jeffrey
Scottsdale
South East Village
Howard & Western
Lincoln Village
115th & Michigan

Commercial developments at and around street intersections can
be classified into two groups depending upon the nature of land uses along
the projecting arteries. On the one hand, commercial developments give
way to non-commercial, usually residential, land uses in all directions.
On the other hand, commercial land uses do not stand in isolation, but
are contiguous with other business activities extending outward along the
projecting arteries. This is especially true where nucleations have
developed at the junction of two or more ribbon developments.

Delimitation of the boundary of a retail nucleation is straight-
forward in the former case but presents a problem in the latter.
Previous researchers have relied heavily upon intuitive notions and
extensive field observation in the construction of boundaries under these
circumstances. However, for the most part, such highly subjective
techniques do not effectively discriminate between nucleated functions
and those typically associated with ribbon developments.[4]

---

[4]For examples of more subjective methods, see M. J. Proudfoot,
"The Major Outlying Business Centers...," op. cit. Proudfoot identified seven different boundary types in delimiting retail nucleations.
They were names according to the type of land use which was excluded
as follows: (a) the neighborhood business boundary; (b) the residential
boundary; (c) the vacant property boundary; (d) the wholesale boundary;
(e) the congregational boundary; (f) the transportational boundary;
(g) the passive boundary. It is interesting to note Proudfoot's comment
that, "Boundaries were based entirely on evidence observed in the field.
Land values were not used since, for the most part, they bore little
relation to specific land use," idem, "The Major Outlying...," op. cit.,
(private edition circulated by the University of Chicago Libraries, 1938),
p. 13. Also see H. M. Mayer, "Generally speaking, boundaries were
placed at points where a nucleated, well defined intensive business
development gives way to a more dispersed, less intensive ribbon
development, to local business use or non-commercial land use such
as railroads, institutional, industrial or residential areas, parks or
vacant land," "Patterns and Recent Trends...," op. cit., p. 8.

In this study, the boundary of a nucleation was drawn at the point of greatest inflection on cross-sectional profiles of land values drawn for both sides of each street leading away from the principal intersection A detailed account of this method and an example of its application are presented in Appendix B. In the few instances where the point of greatest inflection was not clearly identified, boundaries were located after intensive field investigation of retail land uses at those places.[5]

This method of delimitation is preferred by the author for several reasons. Firstly, it affords a way of standardizing the placing of boundaries and thereby enables comparable delimitations from center to center. Secondly, the technique minimizes the degree of subjectivity in decision making on the part of the researcher and thus leads to relatively more objective boundary determination. Thirdly, the method is based on the underlying premise of land value theory. Competition for locations is more intense at the major intersection, where the peak land value occurs. Outward from the intersection along the major streets there is competition for locations, each kind of business seeking to get as near to the major intersection as its rent-paying ability will allow. The result is a gradual decline in land values with increasing distance from the peak intersection. At the boundaries of the nucleations the values of the land approximate those of the long, commercial ribbons which extend for miles along the major streets. It is at this point that nucleated functions give way to those more commonly associated with ribbon developments.

For each ground floor establishment within the boundaries of a retail nucleation, the following measurements were made: (1) type

---

[5] The detailed inventory and delimitation by this method of the 62 retail nucleations included in this work are available in B. J. L. Berry and R. J. Tennant, Chicago Commercial Reference Handbook, (University of Chicago, Department of Geography Research Paper 86, 1963).

of business installed; (2) front foot land value; and (3) floor area in square feet. Summations within each retail nucleation yielded aggregate counts of number of establishments, number of business types and total ground floor space in square feet.[6]

Fundamental Empirical Regularities

The theory of tertiary activity states that high order centers are characterized by more business types and establishments, and it might follow, larger floor areas, than lower order centers. Table 5 indicates the validity of this premise in the study area. Log-linear relationships exist between the number of business types in centers and total floor areas on the one hand, and total number of occupied establishments on the other.[7] Furthermore, a log-log relationship exists between total floor area and number of occupied establishments. Relevant pairwise correlations are significant, and are included with their respective regression equations in Table 5. These relationships are illustrated in Figures 1 and 2, respectively. Also included in Table 5 and Figures 1 and 2 are the corresponding data for the sample of planned shopping centers in the City of Chicago.

Interesting differences are found between the fundamental relationships of the planned centers and those of the unplanned nucleations in respect to the criteria shown. Table 5 shows that log-occupied establishments and total number of business types are more highly correlated in

[6] The Standard Industrial Classification of the Bureau of the Census was used to classify business types. The types identified and their frequency of occurrence at retail nucleations included in the study are given in Appendix C. Land values were obtained from Olcott's Blue Book..., op. cit., and floor area was measured from maps in the Sanborn Atlas but should be considered as approximations of the exact floor space only.

[7] Occupied establishments are used because of the distorting effects of vacant stores.

the planned centers than in the unplanned nucleations. The coefficient
of determination is .92 in the former as opposed to only .84 in the latter.

Conversely, log-floor area and total number of business types show
a higher degree of correlation in the unplanned retail nucleations than
in the planned shopping centers. The coefficient of determination is .75
in the former, compared to only .65 in the latter. Moreover, the overall degree of correlation is much lower between these two variables
than between the log-occupied establishments and number of business
types. This is presumably attributed to the much greater variation in
the ground floor size of establishments within planned shopping centers
as compared to unplanned centers, and greater variability in the size
of retail nucleations in general.

Furthermore, it is noted from the scattergrams, that planned
centers are characterized by markedly different regimes than unplanned
centers. The average numbers of business types, numbers of occupied
establishments and the average floor area (size) are smaller, as reflected in the lower a values, and the rates of change greater, as
reflected in the higher b values, in the regression equations for the
planned shopping centers. Thus, in Figure 1, planned shopping centers
are characterized by fewer establishments than the unplanned retail
nucleations for any given number of business types. This reflects, on
the one hand, the greater degree of functional selection, and on the
other, the lower degree of duplication of functions in planned shopping
centers where only "core" functions are permitted. However, the
wide variation in the size of individual planned shopping centers is
illustrated by the lower correlation coefficient and the greater degree
of scatter about the least squares line in Figure 2. This is explained
by the fact that the size of a shopping center is predetermined in the
planning process, and the size of its constituent establishments fixed
by the level at which the center is to perform.

TABLE 5

SELECTED SIZE RELATIONSHIPS

Correlations (R^2)

	Unplanned			Planned		
	(L.F.A.)	(L.E.)	(B.T.)	(L.F.A.)	(L.E.)	(B.T.)
(L.F.A.) Log. Floor Area	X	.85	.75	X	X	.65
(L.E.) Log. Occupied Establishments		X	.84		X	.92
(B.T.) Business Types			X			X

Regression Equations

Unplanned

1. L.F.A. = 0.0208 (BT) + 1.4466
2. L.E. = 0.0178 (BT) + 1.1860
3. L.F.A. = 1.1451 (LE) + 0.1020

Planned

1. L.F.A. = 0.0326 (BT) + 1.294
2. L.E. = 0.0276 (BT) + 0.8016

34

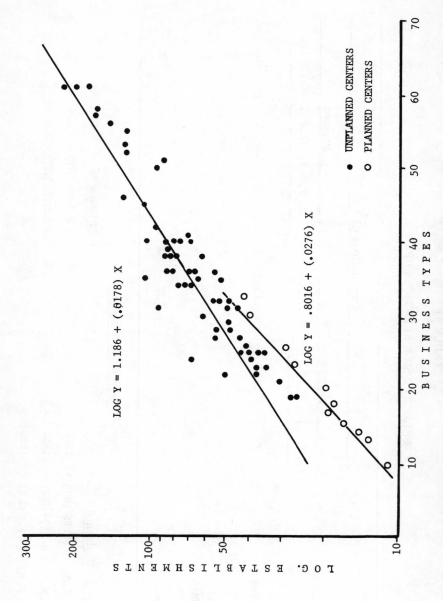

FIGURE 1: REGRESSION OF LOG. OCCUPIED ESTABLISHMENTS ON NUMBER OF BUSINESS TYPES

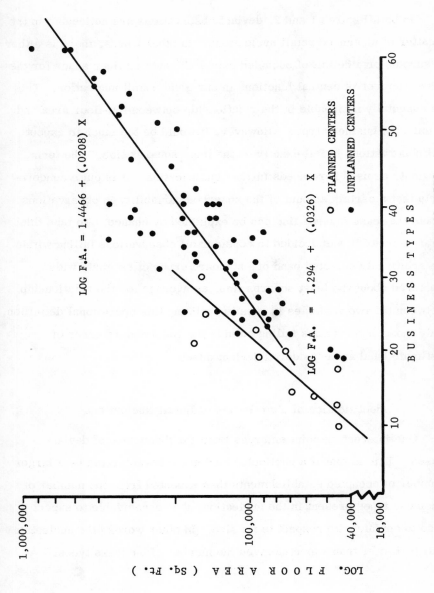

LOG F.A. = 1.4466 + (.0208) X

LOG F.A. = 1.294 + (.0326) X

○ PLANNED CENTERS
● UNPLANNED CENTERS

FIGURE 2: REGRESSION OF LOG. FLOOR AREA ON NUMBER OF BUSINESS TYPES

In both Figures 1 and 2, deviant observations are noticeable in the scatter of unplanned retail nucleations. In other words, there is either a surplus or a deficit of occupied establishments or floor space for the given number of central functions in any given retail nucleation. This is especially noticeable in the relationship between log-floor area and number of business types. However, it would be too much to expect all observations to fall exactly on the least squares line. The term, deviant, as used here needs further qualification. It is quite conceivable that a certain amount of the observed variability in observations about the least squares line can be explained by chance. To take this into account, it was decided to consider all observations falling within an arbitrarily selected band one standard error of estimate wide, centered about the least squares line, as average for the relationship between the two variables in question. Using this operational definition, only those observations falling outside the one standard error of estimate band are considered deviant cases.[8]

Identification of Two Groups of Retail Nucleations

One interesting point emerges from the discussion of deviant cases. This is that if a particular center is characterized by a larger number of occupied establishments than expected from the number of business types present in the nucleation, it is conceivable to expect it also to deviate with respect to its size. In other words, the nucleation will be larger than expected given the number of business types.

[8] For a more refined method of this sort, see E. N. Thomas, "Toward an Expanded Central Place Theory," Geographical Review, 51 (1961), pp. 400-411, and D. Snyder, "The Autonomous-Obsequious Hypothesis of Urban Evolution and its Application to Puerto Rico," (paper presented, A. A. G. meetings, Miami Beach, 1962).

Observations of this type were thought to warrant closer inspection.

The spatial distribution of these retail nucleations deviating noticeably in terms of number of occupied establishments and floor area is illustrated in Figure 3. Comparison of the distribution of deviant nucleations with indices of social and economic "well-being" within the study area reveals a close correspondence between the deviants and those parts of the city currently experiencing decline and socio-economic change, or with the general area of low income (blue collar) population within the study area.[9]

This preliminary, subjective spatial correlation suggests that perhaps two statistical populations exist within the overall study area, the one in the relatively "healthy" parts of the city and the other in the low socio-economic areas. In this event, centers in each area would be characterized by a different set of functional relationships between the variables analyzed. The existence of a dual system is not contrary to the underlying premise of the theory of tertiary activity which is fundamentally based on the magnitude of the available purchasing power in a given tributary area. Consequently, as pointed out in Chapter I, there may well be different systems of central places in urban areas, each related to the socio-economic structure of the tributary areas which they serve.

In order to test this hypothesis, the total number of retail nucleations was disaggregated into two groups: the one comprising

[9] These indices were obtained from the Center for Population Research at the University of Chicago. They included data by census tracts for the percentage of houses built before 1918; percent white collar workers; and an accessibility index based on proximity to adjacent industrial areas. Isoline maps were constructed which enabled the determination of homogeneous areas of low socio-economic status.

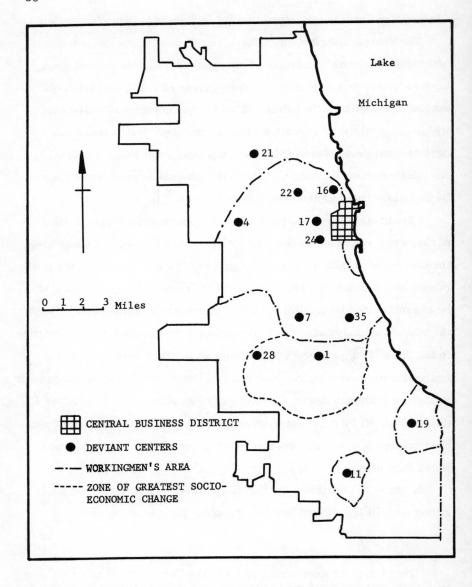

FIGURE 3: RETAIL NUCLEATIONS WITH MORE OCCUPIED ESTABLISHMENTS AND LARGER FLOOR AREA THAN EXPECTED

those nucleations located in an arbitrarily defined low-income area, the other comprising all the remaining centers located in the rest of the city. Tests for differences in the slopes and intercepts of the sub-regression lines using covariance analysis indicate this sub-grouping to be valid. However, there is no significant difference between the slopes of the two regressions, and thus, it cannot be concluded that there are two separate functional relationships in the city. Rather, within the one overall functional relationship, the significant difference in intercepts suggests the existence of two regimes. Each regime comprises a group of nucleations which, in aggregate, differ significantly with respect to mean floor area, mean number of occupied establishments and mean number of business types. The covariance results are shown in Table 6, and the two regimes illustrated in Figures 4 and 5 respectively. Subsequent analysis is based on the existence of these two groups of retail nucleations. For convenience, the group in the low-income area is henceforth referred to as the Workingmen's Centers and the other group, comprising the remainder of the retail nucleations, is referred to as the Rest of the City.

Identification of a Hierarchy of Retail Nucleations

The identification of a hierarchy of retail nucleations within the two areas was based upon further analysis of the relationship between the number of occupied establishments and number of business types. This approach was preferred to the use of floor area data for two reasons. Firstly, retail nucleations are characterized by a high degree of variability in aggregate size as a result of initial differences in the size of their component establishments. In part, this may be due to inaccuracies in the initial measurement. Secondly, numbers of

40

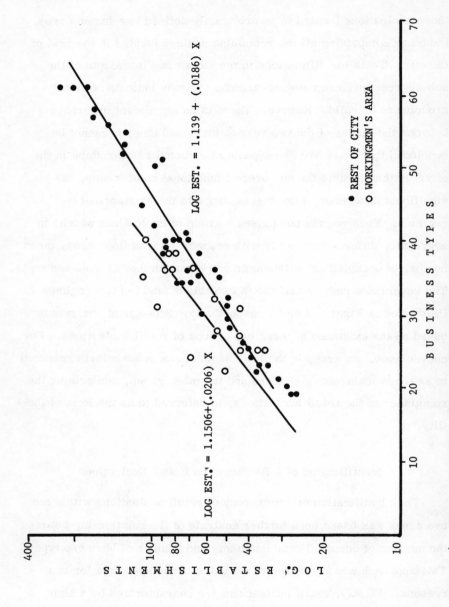

FIGURE 4 : SUB - REGRESSION OF LOG. ESTABLISHMENTS ON NUMBER OF BUSINESS TYPES

LOG EST. = 1.139 + (.0186) X

LOG EST. = 1.1506+(.0206) X

41

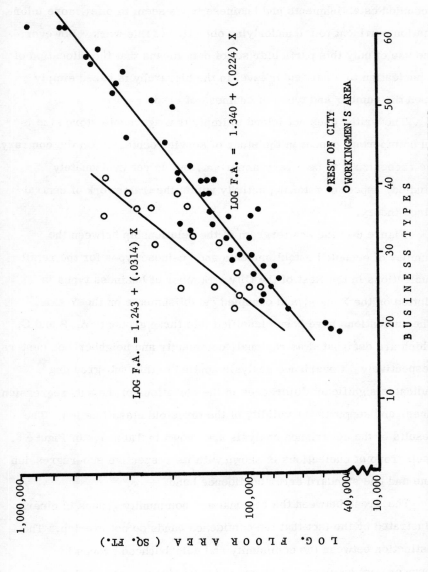

FIGURE 5 : SUB - REGRESSION OF LOG. FLOOR AREA ON NUMBER OF BUSINESS TYPES

LOG F.A. = 1.243 + (.0314) X

LOG F.A. = 1.340 + (.0224) X

● REST OF CITY
○ WORKINGMEN'S AREA

B U S I N E S S   T Y P E S

L O G.   F L O O R   A R E A   (S Q.   F T.)

occupied establishments and business types seem to offer more information pertinent to the underlying objective of this work. However,
the use of only this particular set of data means that the allocation of
a nucleation to a particular level in the hierarchy is based simply
upon the number and types of business offered.

The writer does not intend to imply that aggregate store size is
an unimportant aspect in the study of service centers. On the contrary,
we recognize it to be a very important, but as yet inadequately
studied, aspect of retailing activity within the framework of central
place theory.[10]

Figure 6 is the scattergram of the relationship between the
number of occupied establishments and business types for the retail
nucleations in the Rest of the City. Number of business types is
plotted on the X-axis, and occupied establishments on the Y-axis.
The nucleations have been classified into three groups: A, B and C,
which are designated as regional, community and neighborhood centers
respectively. Covariance analysis applied to this sub-grouping
indicates significant differences in the elevations of the sub-regression
lines, and supports the validity of the threefold classification. The
results of the covariance analysis are shown in Table 7. In Figure 6,
each group of nucleations is shown with its respective sub-regression
line and one standard error confidence band.

The break between the regional and community groups is clearly
illustrated by the fact that the confidence bands do not overlap. The
distinction between the community and neighborhood groups is,
however, not so clear. It becomes increasingly apparent that many

[10] Attention has been called to this problem by B. J. L. Berry,
and W. L. Garrison, "Recent Developments in Central Place Theory,"
op. cit.

TABLE 6

COVARIANCE ANALYSIS ON ELEVATIONS OF SUB-REGRESSION LINES

1. Log Occupied Establishments on Business Types.

Source	Variation	D.f.	Mean Square	F.
Between	.1719	1	.1719	
Within	.3031	59	.0051	33.7

(F. $\propto$ .05 = 4.00)

2. Log Floor Area on Business Types.

Source	Variation	D.f.	Mean Square	F.
Between	.4378	1	.4378	
Within	.7143	59	.0121	36.48**

(F. $\propto$ .05 = 4.00)

** Highly Significant

TABLE 7

COVARIANCE ANALYSIS ON ELEVATIONS OF SUB-REGRESSION LINES
FOR CENTERS IN THE REST OF THE CITY

Log Occupied Establishments on Business

Source	Variation	D.f.	Mean Square	F.
Between	.0362	2	.0181	
Within	.1160	58	.002	9.1**

(F. $\propto$ 0.5 = 4.00)

** Highly Significant

small retail nucleations are associated with values less than the
$750 cut-off point used in the initial identification of retail nucleations.
As a result, these have been omitted from the study. Consequently,
the division into groups B and C -- community and neighborhood
centers -- is based primarily on field observations, is thus quite
subjective, and must for this reason be considered as arbitrary. For
if it should happen that the remaining neighborhood centers assume
the relationship or trend hypothesized in Figure 6, there would be
no justification for distinguishing between the two groups in the manner
indicated. The assumption made here, therefore, in view of lack of
evidence to the contrary, is that the trend line approximates that of
the neighborhood centers shown, and of which only the largest are
included in the study.

Figure 7 (A) contains the basic information concerning the
occupied establishments: business types ratios for the nucleations
in the Workingmen's Area. Instead of the existence of sub-regimes
within the overall relationship, the scattergram reveals a marked
tendency for observations to cluster about the general regression
line. This tendency is more sharply indicated in Figure 7 (B), in
which the axes have been scaled to a common unit of measurement,
with one standard unit of X representing 37 business types and one
standard unit of Y representing 87 occupied establishments. The
X and Y axes have also been rotated to an angle Phi such that the
correlation of X and Y is equal to the cosine of Phi, ($R_{xy} = \cos \phi$).
Since the correlation coefficient is .78, Phi is $38° 4'$. Scaling and
rotation in this manner ensure that direct measurement of distance
between points in the graph is an accurate index of the similarity or
dissimilarity of nucleations not biased by correlation or differing
units of measurement between occupied establishments and numbers

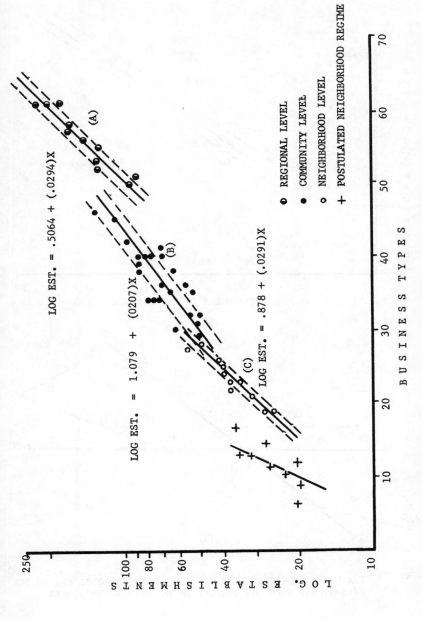

FIGURE 6: SUB - REGRESSIONS OF LOG. ESTABLISHMENTS ON NUMBER OF BUSINESS TYPES FOR DIFFERENT LEVEL CENTERS IN THE REST OF CITY

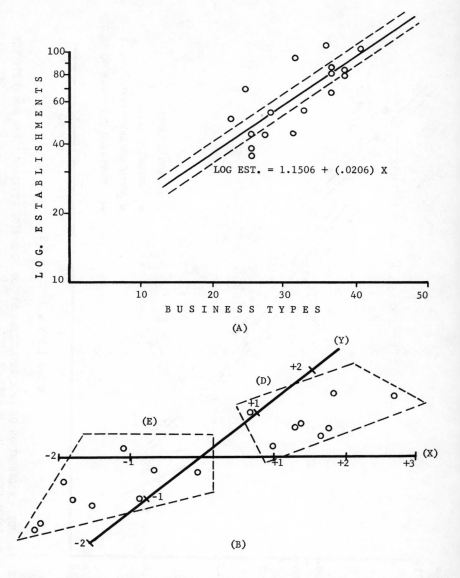

LOG EST. = 1.1506 + (.0206) X

(A)

(B)

FIGURE 7: THE RELATIONSHIP BETWEEN OCCUPIED ESTABLISHMENTS AND NUMBER
OF BUSINESS TYPES AT CENTERS IN THE WORKINGMEN'S AREA

of business types.[11]

Two groups of centers, D and E, are identified from the application of nearest neighbor techniques to the scattergram.[12] Although each group contains those observations that are closer to another member of the group than to any other observation, there is considerable within group distance variation. For convenience at this stage of the analysis, the two groups are called Workingmen's Major (D) and Minor (E), respectively. The results of variance analysis shown in Table 8 indicate a significant difference between the mean number of occupied establishments in the two groups. Variance analysis was also used to test the hypothesis that the mean floor area size of the five groups of centers differs significantly, and Table 9 indicates significant between-group differences.

In summary then, five groups of retail nucleations can be identified within the City of Chicago from an analysis of occupied establishment : business type ratios. Three orders of nucleations are typical of the Rest of the City area, compared to only two orders in the Workingmen's Area. The former nucleations are designated regional, community and neighborhood centers and comprise 11, 23 and 11 nucleations respectively. Each order differs significantly

---

[11] See C. Radhakrishua Rao, "The Utilization of Multiple Measurements in Problems of Biological Classification," Journal of the Royal Statistical Society, Series B (Methods), 10 (1949), pp. 187-188. For an example of the use of the method in a grouping problem, see B. J. L. Berry, "The Impact of Expanding Metropolitan Communities upon the Central Place Hierarchy," Annals of the Association of American Geographers, 50 (1960), pp. 112-116.

[12] For a discussion of nearest neighbor techniques, see M. Dacey, "Analysis of Map Distributions by Nearest Neighbor Methods," Discussion Paper Number 1, (Department of Geography, University of Washington, Seattle, 1958).

48

TABLE 8

VARIANCE ANALYSIS BETWEEN THE LOG. OCCUPIED ESTABLISHMENTS
AND NUMBER OF BUSINESS TYPES FOR CENTERS IN THE WORKINGMEN'S AREA

Source	Variation	D.f.	Variance Estimate	F.
Between	98,476.485	1	98,476.485	
Within	927.31	15	61.8	159.35**
Total	107,749.59	16	---	

** Highly Significant   (F. ∞ 0.5 = 4.54)

TABLE 9

VARIANCE ANALYSIS BETWEEN THE MEAN FLOOR AREA SIZE
OF THE FIVE GROUPS OF RETAIL NUCLEATIONS

Source	Variation	D.f.	Variance Estimate	F.
Between	3.3191	4	0.8298	
Within	1.2913	57	0.0227	36.5**
Total	4.6104	61		

** Highly Significant   (F. ∞ .05 = 2.54)

in the mean number of establishments, business types and floor area (size). The two orders in the Workingmen's areas are designated major and minor centers respectively. These are also significantly different in their mean numbers of occupied establishments, business types and floor area.

The classification offered here is not the only possible allocation of retail nucleations to various levels or orders in a hierarchy. Rather, it may be considered one of several other systems which are dependent upon the methods of analysis and purpose of study. Thus, for example, the analysis of trade areas associated with each center may well indicate that some nucleations do not warrant the order allocated in the above analysis. However, in view of the fact that each of the five groups of retail nucleations is shown to be significantly different from the others, it is deemed acceptable for the purpose of this work. [13]

The Spatial Distribution of the Hierarchies

The spatial distribution of the hierarchy of retail nucleations in the study area is shown in Figure 8, and the address of each center is given in Table 10. Basically, the pattern comprises two distinct clusters, one in the north and the other in the south of the study area. They are separated by a broad band of industrial and transportation land uses. The rectangular grid-iron street pattern has brought about a fairly even spacing of retail nucleations in both areas, with a marked

[13] Thus the classification of centers in B. J. L. Berry, et al, Commercial Structure and Commercial Blight, (Chicago: University of Chicago, Department of Geography, Research Paper 85, 1963) is slightly different from that presented here because of the more powerful grouping technique used.

tendency for the nucleations to be located on the mile section-line and half-section streets, which are the principal traffic arteries and which were significant in the initial development of street car and bus lines.[14] The importance of Madison and of 63rd streets as major shopping arteries is apparent.

The difference between the number of centers in the northern and southern parts of the city is a direct reflection of the basic pattern of population distribution in the City of Chicago. In the south, where approximately one-third of the city population dwells on two-thirds of the land area, there are only 21 nucleations which are, in general, uniformly spaced. On the other hand, the group in the northern part of the city comprises 41 nucleations which serve the remaining two-thirds of the city population.

In general, nucleations of the same order are not uniformly spaced throughout the study area. This is to be expected from the marked unevenness of the population distribution and purchasing power. Furthermore, because centers with peak values of less than $750 per front foot have been omitted in this work, the pattern shown in Figure 8 cannot be viewed as a complete picture of the distribution of retail nucleations. Nevertheless, several generalizations emerge.

The highest level centers -- regional and workingmen's major -- are notably dispersed in their respective parts of the city. The community and workingmen's minor centers exhibit a high degree of spatial clustering within which definite linear orientations are apparent. Both types of centers are quite regularly spaced along certain East-West streets, notably 63rd, Madison and Lawrence.

[14] Mention is made of this in H. M. Mayer, "Patterns and Recent Trends...," op. cit., p. 4.

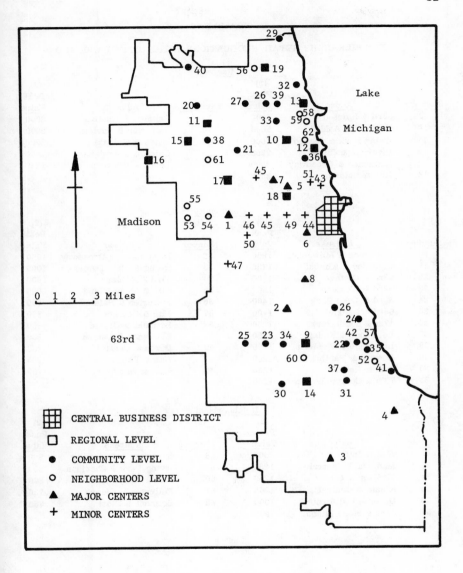

FIGURE 8 : THE HIERARCHY OF RETAIL NUCLEATIONS IN THE CITY OF CHICAGO, 1961

TABLE 10

THE HIERARCHY RETAIL NUCLEATIONS IN THE CITY OF CHICAGO

Regional

(1) Number	Address	(2) Peak Value	(1) Number	Address	(2) Peak Value
9	63rd & Halsted	7000	15	Belmont & Central	2000
10	Belmont & Ashland	5000	16	Fullerton & Harlem	2000
11	Irving Park & Cicero	4000	17	North & Pulaski	2000
12	Diversey & Clark	2750	18	Chicago & Ashland	1600
13	Lawrence & Broadway	2500	19	Devon & Western	1250
14	79th & Halsted	2500			

Community

(1) Number	Address	(2) Peak Value	(1) Number	Address	(2) Peak Value
20	Lawrence & Milwaukee	1800	32	Bryn Mawr & Broadway	1000
21	Diversey & Kimball	1750	33	Irving Park & Damen	1000
22	63rd & Cottage	1750	34	63rd & Ashland	1000
23	63rd & Western	1500	35	67th & Stony Island	1000
24	53rd & Lake Park	1400	36	Fullerton & Halsted	900
25	63rd & Kedzie	1400	37	75th & Cottage	850
26	47th & South Parkway	1200	38	Belmont & Cicero	850
27	Lawrence & Kedzie	1200	39	Lawrence & Damen	800
28	Lawrence & Western	1200	40	Devon & Central	750
29	Howard & Paulina	1200	41	75th & Exchange	750
30	79th & Ashland	1200	42	63rd & Woodlawn	750
31	79th & Cottage Grove	1200			

Neighborhood

(1) Number	Address	(2) Peak Value	(1) Number	Address	(2) Peak Value
52	71st & Jeffrey	2000	58	Montrose & Broadway	800
53	Madison & Central	1250	59	Irving Park & Sheridan	800
54	Madison & Cicero	1250	60	69th & Halsted	800
55	Kinzie & Central	1200	61	Fullerton & Cicero	750
56	Devon & California	1000	62	Belmont & Clark	750
57	63rd & Stony Island	900			

TABLE 10 (Cont'd.)

Workingmen's Major

(1) Number	Address	(2) Peak Value	(1) Number	Address	(2) Peak Value
1	Madison & Pulaski	4000	5	Division & Ashland	1750
2	47th & Ashland	2500	6	Roosevelt & Halsted	1700
3	111th & Michigan	2500	7	North & Milwaukee	1200
4	91st & Commercial	1800	8	35th & Halsted	850

Workingmen's Minor

(1) Number	Address	(2) Peak Value	(1) Number	Address	(2) Peak Value
43	Division & Clark	2000	48	Madison & Western	800
44	Madison & Halsted	2000	49	Madison & Ashland	800
45	North & California	1250	50	Roosevelt & Kedzie	750
46	Madison & Kedzie	1200	51	North & Larrabee	750
47	26th & Pulaski	1100			

NOTE: (1) Numbers are keyed to Figures 8 and 10.

(2) Peak values are given in dollars per front foot.

The neighborhood centers, included in the study area, are mostly concentrated in the northern part of the study area and cluster in close proximity to regional centers. In the case of the three centers at the western edge of the city, they are in close proximity to large suburban shopping centers not shown in the map.

It is interesting to note that certain aspects of the spacing of centers in the city are analogous -- if even of a somewhat rudimentary level -- to findings from studies of the distribution of central places in rural areas. It does raise the possibility that some underlying and fundamental spatial relationship exists in the spacing of different order centers in a hierarchy, regardless of the vast differences in population density and purchasing power between urban and rural areas.

For example, the linear pattern of community and minor centers in the city tends to support Brush's assertion that in rural areas, "lower order centers tend to form rows or belts." Furthermore, the pattern of neighborhood centers appears to support his finding that, "low rank centers tend to crowd together in areas farthest away from the largest centers," while regional centers and in part the major centers offer evidence in the city area of "large centers cluster(ing) more closely to one another."[15]

In spite of the incomplete picture of the distribution of retail nucleations within the city, some evidence is also presented in support of the K = 4 network found by Berry in Iowa.[16] This is not surprising since the rectangular land survey system is characteristic of both —rural and urban Americana. Moreover, the K = 4 network was initially

[15]J. E. Brush, "The Hierarchy of Central Places in Southwestern Wisconsin," The Geographical Review, 43 (1953), pp. 380-402.

[16]B. J. L. Berry and H. M. Mayer, Comparative Studies ...., op. cit., pp. 34-35.

postulated by Christaller to result from strong influence of transportation routes on the system.[17] As has already been noted above, public transportation routes played a very important part in the development of the pattern of retail nucleations in the City of Chicago. An ideal K = 4 network is postulated for the urban area in Figure 9, and although the actual pattern of retail nucleations deviates considerably from this ideal, close inspection reveals a certain measure of agreement.

N	C	N	R	N	C	N	R	N
	N		N		N		N	
N	R	N	C	N	R	N	C	N
	N		N		N		N	
N	C	N	R	N	C	N	R	N
	N		N		N		N	
N	R	N	C	N	R	N	C	N
	N		N		N		N	
N	C	N	R	N	C	N	R	N

R   REGIONAL CENTERS
C   COMMUNITY CENTERS
N   NEIGHBORHOOD CENTERS

FIGURE 9: AN IDEALIZED K = 4 SYSTEM OF RETAIL NUCLEATIONS FOR THE CITY OF CHICAGO

[17] W. Christaller, op. cit.

Summary of the Hierarchies of Retail Nucleations

The fundamental characteristics of the hierarchies of retail nucleations identified in the City of Chicago are shown in Table 11. Regional order centers are characterized by more than fifty business types, and average 147 occupied establishments. Their average size is approximately 400,000 square feet.

TABLE 11

SUMMARY OF FUNDAMENTAL CHARACTERISTICS OF THE HIERARCHY
OF RETAIL NUCLEATIONS IN THE CITY OF CHICAGO, 1961

Characteristic	Rest of City			Workingmen's Area	
	Regional	Community	Neighborhood	Major	Minor
$\bar{X}$ Business Type	55.9	36.9	23.4	36.3	26.6
Range in B.T's	50+	49–29	28–19	40–32	31–22
$\bar{X}$ Occupied Estab.	146.7	72.1	37.5	98.8	47.6
Range Occupied Estab.	220–89	128–48	54–26	180–68	67–35
$\bar{X}$ Floor Area[1]	400,251.8	156,015.0	80,489.0	268,898.7	113,613.3
Range Floor Area(2)	726.9–195.1	297.2–96.5	182.5–43.5	368.3–172.6	163.2–87.3
$\bar{X}$ Store Size[3]	2,674.6	2,158.2	1,888.6	3,083.6	2,450.2
Numbers	11	23	11	8	9

NOTES: (1) Floor area measured in square feet.
        (2) In 000's square feet.
        (3) Including only occupied stores, measured in square feet.

Community order centers have between 29 and 49 business types, but average only 72 occupied establishments. However, the larger community centers may have as many business types as the smaller regional centers. They are considerably smaller than the latter, with 156,015 square feet, and average about two-fifths the size of regional centers.

Neighborhood centers have between 19 and 28 business types, with an average of 23, about half as many as the regional centers. They have roughly one quarter the number of establishments of a regional center. However, within group variability results in some overlap with smaller community centers. With an average floor area of 80,500 square feet, they are about one-half as large as the community centers. This rather large size is to be expected since only the largest neighborhood centers have been included in the study.

In the Workingmen's Area, the major centers have an average of 36 business types, ranging between 32 and 40. With 99 occupied establishments they are somewhat smaller than the regional centers in the Rest of the City. Their average size is about 269,000 square feet. On the other hand, minor centers have an average of only 27 business types, and range between 22 and 31. They have approximately half as many occupied establishments, 47, as the major centers. This is a similar proportion shown by that in community to regional centers in the Rest of the City. They are just under half the size of the major centers, with an average area of 113,600 square feet.[18]

[18] It is interesting to note the similarities between these figures and those for planned centers presented by H. Hoyt in, "Classification and Significant Characteristics of Shopping Centers," Appraisal Journal, April 1958, pp. 214-222.

It is interesting to compare the centers in the Workingmen's Area with those of the Rest of the City in terms of the basic characteristics so far considered. Firstly, there seems to be a close correspondence in the relative positions of the community and minor centers to the regional and major centers, respectively. The two lower order centers have about half the number of occupied establishments and floor area of the highest order centers. Secondly, the major and minor centers appear to be similar to the community and neighborhood centers, respectively. This is especially true of the average number of business types. In respect to the number of occupied establishments and floor area, major centers lie somewhere between the regional and community order centers, and in general approximate the largest of the community level group. The minor centers show a similar kind of relationship to the larger neighborhood/ smaller community level centers.

CHAPTER III

THE FUNCTIONAL STRUCTURE OF RETAIL NUCLEATIONS

The classification of retail nucleations proposed in the previous chapter was based solely upon numbers of establishments and business types. No account was taken of the specific types offered from each center. We now turn to an analysis of the functional structure of each group of centers to determine the viability of the proposed classification.

Classification of Central Functions

In the above analysis, the total number of business types at a nucleation includes any business and service activity listed in the S.I.C. classification. Consequently, the total count of business types includes a wide variety of functions which do not require central locations. For example, representatives of the automobile group of functions and such infrequently demanded services as electrical repairs are more typical of urban arterial locations than retail nucleations. It is now appropriate to consider only those business types that are basic to the role of a retail nucleation as a central place. These are

59

henceforth called central functions. Accordingly, sixty-four functions are considered central in locational requirements. These are listed in Table 12. The selection of these is based upon field observation and the findings of other researchers.[1]

Several shortcomings in the S. I. C. classification should be mentioned at this point. First, and most importantly, the classification is essentially based on single product firms. In the real world however, most retail establishments engage in more than one category of business, and are thus more correctly viewed as offering a "bundle of goods" to the customer. The lack of sophistication of the single-product approach has been pointed out by Holton, who argues for a more realistic theory of retailing couched in terms of a multi-product firm.[2]

Second, since the S. I. C. classification does not identify differences in quality, it assumes a perfectly competitive system. This is opposed to the more realistic situation of imperfect competition arising from the notions of product differentiation. Although these shortcomings are recognized here, exploration of substitute systems of classification lie outside the general scope of this work, and for convenience, establishments are categorized in this study according to their dominant line.

A further point apropos levels of aggregation of individual elements

[1]In part on the work of B. J. L. Berry, "Shopping Centers...," op. cit., and in part on the proposals of B. J. L. Berry and R. M. Lillibridge, "Guides for the Provision of Shopping Centers and Allied Service Districts in Residential Communities," (unpublished draft copy, Community Renewal Program, City of Chicago, 1962).

[2]R. H. Holton, op. cit. Berry argues that central place theory is compatible with the equilibrium conditions proposed by Holton if each level of the hierarchy is imagined to function as a firm. See B. J. L. Berry and W. L. Garrison, "Recent Developments...," op. cit.

TABLE 12
CENTRAL FUNCTIONS

S.I.C. Code		S.I.C. Code	
5231	Paint & glass	5732	Radio & T.V.
5251	Hardware	5733	Music stores
5311	Department stores	5812	Eating places
5331	Variety	5813	Bars
5392	Army & navy	5912	Drug stores
'10	Supermarket	"5932	Antique stores
5411	Grocery	5921	Liquor stores
5422	Meat markets	"5933	Secondhand clothing
5423	Fish	"5934	Secondhand furniture
5441	Candy	5942	Books
5462	Bakeries	5943	Stationery
5499	Delicatessen	5952	Sporting goods
5612	Men's & boys' clothing	5971	Jewelry stores
5621	Women's clothing	5992	Florists
5631	Millinery	5993	Cigar stores
5632	Lingerie	5996	Cameras
5633	Hosiery	5997	Gift & novelty
5634	Apparel accessory	5999	Miscellaneous retail
5641	Children's wear	60	Banks
5651	Family clothing	605	Currency exchange
5662	Men's shoes	6159	Loans (personal)
5663	Women's shoes	64	Insurance agents
5664	Children's shoes	65	Real Estate agents
5665	Family shoes	7211	Dry cleaners
5681	Furriers	7215	Laundomats
5699	Miscellaneous Apparel	7221	Photographers
5712	Furniture	7231	Beauty shops
5713	Floor covering	7241	Barbers
5714	Drapery	7251	Shoe repairs
5715	China & glassware	7631	Watch repairs
5719	Miscellaneous Furnishings	783	Motion picture theaters
5722	Appliances	7949	Sports promoters
5431	Fruit & vegetables	801	Medical services
		8099	Optometrist

Notes: '10 - University of Chicago code number
"59 - Secondhand stores are not considered as central functions in the Rest of the City area, but are considered central in the Workingmen's Area.

in the classification needs to be mentioned. Three levels are used
here. First, generalizations are based on individual central functions
in the classification, for example, women's clothing stores, meat
markets, etc.; second, they are based on the aggregation of several
functions within any one major S.I.C. group, for example, the food,
clothing, or furniture groups; third, generalizations are based on the
distinction between convenience, shopping and other central goods. [3]

Sample Procedure

A representative random sample of the sixty-two retail nucleations
is used as the basis for the analysis of functional structure and subsequent analysis of the relationship between central functions and land
values. A modified stratified random sample was preferred to select
the number of sample cases proportional to the total number of centers
comprising each of the five groups. Fifty percent of the total regional
group, and twenty-five percent of the centers in the four other categories were sampled. A higher proportion was selected from the regional
group because the relationship between store location and land value is
more fully developed at that level. The sample included five regional
centers, six community level centers, and three each from the neighborhood, Workingmen's major and minor centers, respectively. The
distribution of the sample centers is shown in Figure 10, and the address
of each, together with its peak land value, is given in Table 13.

Allocation of Functions by Level

A variety of methods, varying in degree of sophistication, are
available to allocate and identify central functions typical of different

[3]The Bureau of the Census included the following S. I. C. major
groups of functions in shopping, convenience and other goods respectively: 54--, 58-- and 5912; 53--, except 5322, 56-- and 57--; the
remainder of functions classified.

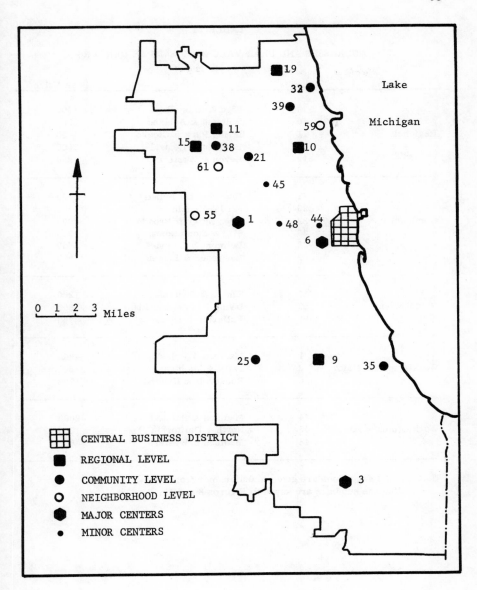

FIGURE 10: THE DISTRIBUTION OF SAMPLE RETAIL NUCLEATIONS

TABLE 13

ADDRESSES AND PEAK VALUES OF SAMPLE CENTERS

Level	Number[2]	Address	Peak Value[1]
Regional	9	63rd & Halsted	7000
	10	Belmont & Ashland	5000
	11	Irving Park & Cicero	4000
	15	Belmont & Central	2000
	19	Devon & Western	1250
Community	21	Diversey & Kimball	1750
	25	63rd & Kedzie	1400
	32	Bryn Mawr & Broadway	1000
	35	67th & Stony Island	1000
	38	Belmont & Cicero	850
	39	Lawrence & Damen	800
Neighborhood	55	Kinzie & Central	1200
	59	Irving Park & Sheridan	800
	61	Fullerton & Cicero	750
Workingmen's Major	1	Madison & Pulaski	4000
	3	111th & Michigan	2500
	6	Roosevelt & Halsted	1700
Workingmen's Minor	44	Madison & Halsted	2000
	45	North & California	1250
	48	Madison & Western	800

Notes: (1) Peak values are given in dollars per front foot.
(2) The numbers are keyed to Figures 8 and 10.

levels in a hierarchy.[4] A more subjective method is used here. Allocation is based in part on a modification of recent proposals by the Community Renewal Program of the City of Chicago,[5] in part on the findings of other research,[6] and from the author's own field experience and data analysis.

As we have pointed out above, functions are not distributed among centers in the urban area with anything like the steplike regularity typical of rural areas. Consequently, the identification of functions typical of the different levels in an hierarchy is rather more difficult, and calls for more rigorous methods of analysis. Variability in the distribution of functions among centers can be taken into account if certain functions are considered as comprising the "core" of a nucleation at a given level, whilst others are considered as only optional. The "core" functions are those considered basic to the functioning of a nucleation at a given level in a hierarchy, whereas optional functions, present in varying numbers and combinations, are dependent upon the availability of rentable space, and the social and economic requirements of the trade areas they serve.

[4] For example, in a recent study factor analysis was used, see B. J. L. Berry, Comparative Studies of Central Place Systems, op. cit. Cluster analysis was used by R. Mayfield in "Conformations of Service and Retail Activities: an Example in Lower Orders of an Urban Hierarchy in a Lesser Developed Area," The I. G. U. Symposium in Urban Geography, (Lund: C. W. Gleerup, 1962), pp. 77-89.

[5] B. J. L. Berry and R. M. Lillibridge, op. cit.

[6] B. J. L. Berry and H. M. Mayer, op. cit., and B. J. L. Berry, "Ribbon Developments in the Urban Business Pattern," Annals of the Association of American Geographers, 49 (1959), pp. 146-155.

Analysis of Functions by Level of Center

Neighborhood Centers

Functions typical of this level are essentially the convenience
kind. They are identified by the S. I. C. identification code, together
with their frequency of occurrence at neighborhood centers in Table 14.
Seventeen functions are included; eight of which comprise the "core",
while the remainder are considered optional.[7] Five of the eight "core"
functions are fully represented at this level. They include groceries,
bakeries, eating places, bars and drug stores. In addition, half of the
optional types are fully represented, including currency exchanges,
real estate agents, barber and beauty shops and basic medical services.[8] The other functions at this level are represented in at least
two-thirds of the sample centers.

One rather interesting feature at this level is the anomolous
occurrence in all centers of variety stores, which are considered a
community level function. Field investigation offers a partial explanation for this. Although they constitute variety stores in terms of the
S. I. C. classification, they usually offer only a limited range of goods
and could perhaps be considered more correctly as large general
stores. However, given the extreme within-group variability in size
of center at this level, the presence of small limited price variety
stores is expected since only the larger neighborhood level centers are
included in the study.

[7] Five of these "core" functions are classified in the S. I. C. convenience category; the two other functions are personal services which
although basically convenience in type, are for some reason not included by the Census Bureau in this category.

[8] In Chapter I, currency exchanges were stated as typical of the
community level centers according to B. J. L. Berry's investigations
in Snohomish County, Washington. In the City of Chicago, they are
considered typical of the lower neighborhood centers.

TABLE 14

NEIGHBORHOOD LEVEL FUNCTIONS

S.I.C. Code	Description	Frequency[1]
5251	Hardware	1
5411 (+)	Grocery	3
10	Supermarkets	2
5422 (+)	Meat markets	2
5423	Fish markets	0
5462 (+)	Bakeries	3
5812 (+)	Eating places	3
5813 (+)	Bars	3
5912 (+)	Drug stores	3
605	Currency exchange	3
65	Real estate agents	3
7211 (+)	Dry cleaners	2
7215 (+)	Laundromats	2
7231	Beauty shops	3
7241	Barbers	3
7251	Shoe repairs	2
80---	Medical services	3

Notes: (+) indicates "core" functions.
(1) The frequency number says that, for example, grocery stores appear in all three sample centers at this level.

The types of functions and number of establishments at each sample center are shown in Table 15. Many higher order functions are found at this level illustrating the more complex distribution of functions at centers in the urban area. Although store quality is not investigated in this work, cursory field observation suggests that these are perhaps of lower quality than similar stores at higher level centers.

The average percent composition of neighborhood centers is shown in Table 16 by S.I.C. major groups. The table clearly reveals the dominance of convenience functions. This group accounts for over one-third of all establishments. The largest single representatives are the eating and drinking (58) and the personal service (72) groups, which account for 22.4 and 20.2 percent of establishments, respectively. Shopping goods appear unimportant; the clothing group (56) and the furniture group (57) account for only 4.0 and 1.5 percent of establishments, respectively. The 10.8 percent attributed to the miscellaneous group (59) is fairly evenly divided between drug stores and liquor stores.

Community Centers

The twenty-four functions typical of this level and their frequency of occurrence in sample centers are shown in Table 17. Eleven are considered "core" functions, and the remaining fourteen are considered optional. It should be remembered that theoretically all the neighborhood level functions are found at this level, and so they, too, constitute "core" elements. In general, centers at this level are characterized by a greater number and duplication of functions, and arising from this, greater variability in functional structure. Surprisingly, however, "core" functions are represented only in about half of the centers.

TABLE 15

THE FUNCTIONAL STRUCTURE OF NEIGHBORHOOD LEVEL SAMPLE CENTERS

S. I. C. Code	Description	Frequency			
		(1)	(2)	(3)	(4)
5251	Hardware	1	–	–	1
5331	Variety	1	1	1	3
5411 (+)	Grocery	2	2	2	6
10	Supermarkets	2	1	–	3
5422 (+)	Meat markets	1	–	1	2
5441	Candy	–	1	–	1
5462 (+)	Bakeries	1	1	1	3
5612	Men's & boys' clothing	1	1	–	2
5621	Women's clothing	1	–	–	1
5632	Lingerie	–	1	–	1
5681	Furriers	1	–	–	1
5732	Radio & T. V.	1	1	–	2
5812 (+)	Eating places	9	6	3	18
5813 (+)	Bars	6	3	2	11
5912 (+)	Drug stores	2	1	2	5
5921	Liquor stores	4	1	–	5
5971	Jewelry stores	–	–	1	1
5992	Florists	–	1	–	1
5997	Gift & novelty	1	1	–	2
60	Banks	–	1	–	1
605	Currency exchanges	1	1	1	3
6159	Loans (personal)	–	1	1	2
65	Real estate agents	1	3	4	8
7211 (+)	Dry cleaners	6	5	–	11
7215 (+)	Laundromats	3	2	–	5
7231	Beauty shops	1	1	1	3
7241	Barbers	3	1	1	5
7251	Shoe repairs	1	–	1	2
7631	Watch repairs	1	1	–	2
783	Motion picture theaters	–	1	–	1
801	Medical services	1	1	2	4
8099	Optometrists	–	1	1	2
Vacant		3	2	–	5

Notes: (1) Irving Park and Sheridan
(2) Kinzie and Central
(3) Fullerton and Cicero
(4) Total number of functions in sample centers.
(+) Indicates "core" functions.

TABLE 16

PERCENTAGE COMPOSITION OF LEVEL OF CENTER BY S. I. C. GROUPS

S. I. C.[1]	Percent Establishments				
	N.	C.	R.	Ma.	Mi.
52-	1.5	2.0	0.8	1.6	0.6
53-	2.3	5.0	3.5	5.5	1.3
54-	11.6	9.1	6.7	8.6	9.0
56-	4.0	14.4	25.0	38.0	16.0
57-	1.5	6.0	11.0	10.0	4.2
58-	22.4	15.0	9.0	8.4	23.2
59-	10.8	14.2	14.1	10.0	14.3
72-	20.2	13.7	9.0	1.8	10.2
Other central functions (2)	17.8	9.0	8.4	5.2	11.0
Vacant	4.0	6.2	8.0	8.4	6.2
Non-central functions (3)	3.9	5.4	4.5	2.4	4.2
TOTAL	100.0	100.0	100.0	100.0	100.0

Notes: (1) The S. I. C. groups comprise all individual elements classified by the first two digits of the S. I. C. code.

(2) Other central functions include all other types of which only one element is characterized by the first two digits of the S. I. C. code; for example, 783 (motion picture theaters), etc. .

(3) Non-central functions include all business types present in nucleations although not considered as typical of retail nucleations in this study; for example, automobile functions, etc. .

TABLE 17

COMMUNITY LEVEL FUNCTIONS

S. I. C. Code	Description	Frequency[1]
5231	Paint, glass, etc.	3
5311 (+)	Department stores	4
5331 (+)	Variety	5
5392	Army & navy stores	2
5431	Fruit & vegetables	1
5441 (+)	Candy	5
5499	Delicatessen	3
5612 (+)	Men's & boys' clothing	4
5621 (+)	Women's clothing	4
5651	Family clothing	2
5665 (+)	Family shoe stores	5
5712	Furniture	5
5732	Radio & T. V.	5
5733	Records & music	3
5921 (+)	Liquor stores	5
5943 (+)	Stationery	3
5992	Florists	3
5997 (+)	Gift & novelty	3
5971 (+)	Jewelry	4
60 (+)	Banks	3
6159	Personal loans	3
7631	Watch repairs	0
783	Motion picture theaters	4
80-- (2)	Medical services	6

Notes: (1) The maximum frequency at this level is 6, there being six centers included in the sample.

(2) Medical services are included also as functions typical of the neighborhood level; since the medical group is not differentiated, it is implied that more specialized medical services are offered at this level.

(+) Indicates "core" functions.

The types of central functions and number of establishments at sample centers are listed in Table 18. In general, centers at this level are functionally more complex than the lower level neighborhood centers. A significant feature is the notable increase in variety and department stores. There is also a notable increase in the number of hardware stores and supermarkets which, although classified as neighborhood functions, did not appear to be typical at that level. In the case of the latter, this is presumably related to their large scale operation and their higher thresholds which cannot be satisfied at the neighborhood level. The frequent occurrence of candy stores reflects the increased concentration of shoppers at this level of center. Since candy stores depend upon compulsive purchasing by the consumer, they tend to maximize their location with respect to high pedestrian counts.

The average percent composition of community centers by S. I. C. major groups is shown in Table 16. The large increase in the shopping group stands out as the most striking difference between this and the lower level centers. In particular, the proportion of the clothing group (56) is significantly higher, accounting for 14.4 percent of establishments. There is also a notable increase in the furniture group (57) which accounts for 6.0 percent of establishments, and in the miscellaneous group (59) which increases to 14.2 percent at this level. Conversely, there is a marked decrease in the proportion of establishments devoted to the eating and drinking group (58), personal services (72) and other central functions, which account for only 15.0, 20.2 and 9.0 percent of establishments, respectively.

Regional Centers

Central functions typical of this level in the hierarchy, together with their frequency of occurrence in sample centers are listed in Table 19. It is to be noted that no "core" functions are identified at this level. Rather, centers are characterized by varying numbers of more specialized types in addition to a larger number and greater duplication of all lower level functions. Twenty-three new functions are added at this level. Over half of all the central functions are fully represented, indicating the more complete functional structure of centers at this level.

The types and numbers of establishments in each sample regional center are shown in Table 20. The basic structure of regional centers comprises three or four major department stores, several variety stores, and a complete range of clothing, apparel accessory, shoe, furniture and appliance stores. Functions occurring only at this level include the more specialized members of the clothing and furniture groups, such as millinery, lingerie, hosiery, jewelers, children's wear, glassware, drapery, floor covering, household appliances, and camera and sporting goods stores. Photographic studios and optometrists are typical. The apparent paucity of other medical services at this level is explained by the fact that they tend to occupy upper floor locations at centers of this size.

The average composition by S.I.C. major groups is shown for this level in Table 16. There is a notable increase in both the clothing (56) and furniture (57) groups, which together account for over one-third of all establishments. With the exception of the increased proportion of vacancies at this level, all other groups show a smaller proportion of establishments than at the lower level community centers. The decrease is most marked in the eating and drinking group (58) and the food group (54), which only account for 9.0 percent and 6.7 percent of establishments, respectively. The food (54), eating and drinking (58) and personal service (72) groups are characterized by a consistent decline in the proportion of establishments at each succeeding higher level in the hierarchy, and are represented

TABLE 18

THE FUNCTIONAL STRUCTURE OF
COMMUNITY LEVEL SAMPLE CENTERS

S. I. C. Code	Description	Frequency						
		(1)	(2)	(3)	(4)	(5)	(6)	(7)
5231	Paint & Glass	–	1	1	–	1	–	3
5251	Hardware	1	2	1	1	–	2	7
5311 (+)	Department stores	4	–	1	1	–	2	8
5331 (+)	Variety	3	1	2	1	–	5	12
5392	Army & Navy	–	–	–	1	–	2	3
5411	Grocery	–	1	4	3	–	1	9
10	Supermarkets	2	4	1	2	1	2	12
5422	Meat Markets	2	2	–	–	1	–	5
5431	Fruit & vegetables	1	–	–	–	–	–	1
5441 (+)	Candy	2	1	–	1	1	3	8
5462	Bakeries	1	2	1	–	1	1	6
5499	Delicatessen	1	–	–	1	1	–	3
5612 (+)	Men's & boys' clothes	5	1	1	–	–	3	10
5621 (+)	Women's clothes	6	5	3	–	–	8	22
5631	Millinery	–	1	–	1	–	–	2
5634	Apparel accessory	–	–	1	–	–	–	1
5641	Children's wear	2	1	–	1	–	3	7
5651	Family clothes	2	–	–	–	–	2	4
5662	Men's shoes	2	–	–	–	–	–	2
5663	Women's shoes	3	–	–	–	–	–	3
5665	Family shoes	5	1	4	1	–	4	15
5699	Miscellaneous Apparel	2	–	–	–	–	–	2
5712	Furniture	1	–	2	1	1	2	7
5713	Floor covering	–	–	1	1	–	–	2
5714	Drapery	1	1	–	–	–	1	3
5715	China & glassware	–	–	–	–	–	1	1
5719	Miscellaneous furnishings	–	1	–	–	–	1	2
5722	Appliances	1	2	–	–	–	–	3
5732	Radio & T. V.	–	2	2	1	1	1	7
5733	Music stores	2	–	1	–	–	1	4
5812	Eating places	7	10	9	5	5	7	43
5813	Bars	–	9	9	4	5	1	28
5912	Drug stores	3	3	4	2	2	4	18

TABLE 18 - Continued

S.I.C. Code	Description	Frequency						
		(1)	(2)	(3)	(4)	(5)	(6)	(7)
5921 (+)	Liquor stores	1	3	3	1	2	0	10
5932	Antique stores	-	1	-	-	-	-	1
5933	Secondhand clothing	-	-	1	-	-	-	1
5934	Secondhand furniture	-	-	1	-	-	-	1
5942	Books	-	1	-	-	-	-	1
5943 (+)	Stationery	-	1	-	-	1	1	3
5952	Sporting goods	-	-	1	-	-	1	2
5971 (+)	Jewelry stores	2	-	-	1	2	4	9
5992	Florists	-	1	1	2	-	-	4
5993	Cigar stores	-	-	1	-	-	-	1
5996	Cameras	1	-	-	1	-	-	2
5997 (+)	Gift & novelty	4	-	2	-	3	-	9
5999	Miscellaneous retail	1	2	-	2	-	1	6
60 (+)	Banks	-	-	1	-	1	1	3
605	Currency exchange	-	2	2	1	1	1	7
6159	Loans (personal)	-	-	2	1	1	-	4
64	Insurance agents	-	-	-	-	-	1	1
65	Real estate agents	-	2	2	2	2	1	9
7211	Dry cleaners	1	10	7	3	2	-	23
7215	Laundromats	1	2	2	2	1	-	8
7221	Photographers	-	-	-	-	1	-	1
7231	Beauty shops	3	5	1	4	3	3	19
7241	Barbers	-	1	5	1	2	-	9
7251	Shoe repairs	-	3	1	1	-	1	6
783	Motion picture theaters	1	1	2	-	-	1	5
801	Medical services	-	1	-	2	1	1	5
8099	Optometrists	3	-	1	3	2	-	9
Vacant		9	4	7	2	4	4	30

Notes: (1) Diversey and Kimball
(2) Bryn Mawr and Broadway
(3) 67th and Stony Island
(4) Lawrence and Damen
(5) Belmont and Cicero
(6) 63rd and Kedzie
(7) Total establishments of each function in the sample centers.
(+) Indicates "core" functions.

least of all at regional centers. There is virtually the same proportion of the miscellaneous group (59) at this level as at the community
level, but it should be remembered that the individual types comprising this group are somewhat different in the regional centers.

TABLE 19

REGIONAL LEVEL FUNCTIONS

S.I.C. Code	Description	Frequency[1]
5631	Millinery	4
5632	Lingerie	3
5633	Hosiery	3
5634	Apparel accessories	3
5641	Children's wear	5
5662	Men's shoes	5
5663	Women's shoes	5
5664	Children's shoes	2
5681	Furriers	0
5699 (2)	Miscellaneous apparel	2
5715	China & glassware	2
5714	Drapery	4
5713	Floor covering	3
5719 (3)	Miscellaneous furnishings	3
5722	Appliances	4
5942	Books	0
5952	Sporting goods	4
5993	Cigar stands	0
5996	Camera shops	5
5999 (4)	Miscellaneous retail	5
64	Insurance agents	2
7221	Photographic studies	4
7949 (5)	Sports promoters	4

Notes: (1) The maximum frequency at this level is five.
  (2) This group comprises specialized clothing stores such as
      tie shops, etc.
  (3) This group includes infrequently found specialized furniture
      stores.
  (4) Including such things as health foods and religious goods, etc.
  (5) This group includes bowling alleys, billiard and pool halls,
      etc.

Workingmen's Centers

It is expected that these centers will be characterized by functions
reflecting the nature of demand associated with the lower income area
in which they are located. They should, however, be ordered in the
same way as the centers in the Rest of the City. The diminished level
of purchasing power should be reflected in the absence of certain kinds
of specialized high threshold functions. On the other hand, they should
be characterized by stores offering goods purchased more frequently
by low income groups, especially the convenience types, and by a
greater proportion of more general types of functions.

The types of functions and number of establishments in the minor
centers are listed in Table 21. Ten functions are fully represented.
These are candy stores, men's clothing and shoes, eating and drinking,
drug and liquor stores, jewelers, barber shops and motion picture
theaters. Although jewelry stores are well represented, they are of
lower quality than those found at centers in the Rest of the City. Field
investigation indicates that there is an increase in the amount of cheap-
er costume jewelry offered from these stores.

The lower level of demand in the area is perhaps reflected in the
large number of family clothing stores as opposed to the occurrence of
the more specialized types. Moreover, secondhand stores appear more
frequently than in centers in the Rest of the City, and there is a notable
concentration of bars and eating places which tend to give the centers
a "skid row" character, especially in those areas recently taken over
by immigrant groups.

The functional structure of major centers is shown in Table 22.
Fifteen functions are fully represented. In addition to a duplication of
types found in the minor centers, there is an increase in variety and
department stores, furniture, drapery, appliance, women's clothing,
family shoe, gift and novelty stores, banking and medical services.

TABLE 20

THE FUNCTIONAL STRUCTURE OF REGIONAL LEVEL SAMPLE CENTERS

S.I.C. Code	Description	Frequency					
		(1)	(2)	(3)	(4)	(5)	(6)
5231	Paint & glass	1	2	-	-	1	4
5251	Hardware	-	-	2	2	-	4
5311	Department stores	1	3	2	3	3	12
5331	Variety	3	3	2	3	3	14
5392	Army and navy	-	2	1	3	1	7
5411	Grocery	2	-	1	3	2	8
10	Supermarkets	-	3	-	3	3	9
5422	Meat markets	2	3	2	4	1	12
5423	Fish	1	-	-	-	-	1
5431	Fruit & vegetables	-	-	-	-	1	1
5441	Candy	4	2	3	4	2	15
5462	Bakeries	1	3	1	3	-	8
5499	Delicatessens	1	3	1	2	-	7
5612	Men's & boys' clothes	4	4	9	9	10	36
5621	Women's clothes	3	23	20	13	16	75
5631	Millinery	-	1	2	1	2	6
5632	Lingerie	2	1	-	1	-	4
5633	Hosiery	1	-	-	2	2	5
5634	Apparel accessory	1	1	-	1	-	3
5641	Children's wear	2	4	3	2	5	16
5651	Family clothes	1	-	1	2	4	8
5662	Men's shoes	1	2	3	3	3	12
5663	Women's shoes	2	2	3	7	7	21
5664	Children's shoes	1	1	-	-	-	2
5665	Family shoes	2	6	5	7	11	31
5699	Miscellaneous apparel	-	2	-	-	2	4
5712	Furniture	2	8	9	16	11	46
5713	Floor covering	-	2	2	3	-	7
5714	Drapery	-	2	3	2	4	11
5715	China & glassware	-	1	1	-	-	2
5719	Miscellaneous furnishings	-	1	1	-	2	4
5722	Appliances	-	3	3	1	2	9
5732	Radio & T.V.	2	-	4	5	1	12
5733	Music stores	1	1	1	5	3	11
5812	Eating places	5	9	11	14	15	54
5813	Bars	1	3	5	6	14	29
5912	Drug stores	4	4	4	4	4	20

TABLE 20 - Continued

S.I.C. Code	Description	Frequency					
		(1)	(2)	(3)	(4)	(5)	(6)
5921	Liquor stores	1	4	2	2	4	13
5933	Secondhand clothing	-	-	-	-	2	2
5939	Secondhand stores not elsewhere classified	-	-	-	-	3	3
5943	Stationery	1	2	1	2	1	7
5952	Sporting goods	-	1	5	1	2	9
5971	Jewelry stores	3	6	6	7	11	33
5992	Florists	-	2	-	1	1	4
5996	Cameras	1	1	2	2	1	7
5997	Gift & novelty	2	4	5	5	2	18
5999	Miscellaneous retail	6	2	2	1	3	14
60	Banks	1	2	2	1	1	7
605	Currency exchange	1	2	1	2	2	8
6159	Loans (personal)	2	5	4	3	4	18
64	Insurance agents	-	1	-	-	2	3
65	Real estate agents	1	-	2	2	2	7
7211	Dry cleaners	3	4	1	2	5	15
7215	Laundromats	1	3	2	1	4	11
7221	Photographers	2	1	-	1	1	5
7231	Beauty shops	2	6	5	6	5	24
7241	Barbers	3	3	5	2	5	18
7251	Shoe repairs	-	2	2	-	5	9
7631	Watch repairs	-	-	-	1	-	1
783	Motion picture theaters	1	1	1	-	4	7
7949	Sports promoters	1	1	1	2	-	5
801	Medical services	1	-	1	1	-	3
8099	Optometrists	2	3	4	7	3	19
Vacant		9	13	8	11	33	74

Notes: (1) Devon and Western
(2) Belmont and Central
(3) Irving Park and Cicero
(4) Belmont and Ashland
(5) 63rd and Halsted
(6) Total establishments of each function in the sample centers

TABLE 21

THE FUNCTIONAL STRUCTURE OF WORKINGMEN'S MINOR SAMPLE CENTERS

S.I.C. Code	Description	Frequency			
		(1)	(2)	(3)	(4)
5251	Hardware	–	–	1	1
5331	Variety	1	–	–	1
5392	Army & Navy	1	–	–	1
5411	Grocery	–	1	–	1
10	Supermarkets	2	–	–	2
5422	Meat markets	–	–	1	1
5423	Fish	1	–	–	1
5431	Fruit & vegetables	–	–	1	1
5441	Candy	2	1	1	4
5462	Bakeries	2	–	–	2
5499	Delicatessen	1	–	–	1
5612	Men's & boys' clothes	1	3	5	9
5621	Women's clothes	1	–	–	1
5631	Millinery	–	1	–	1
5641	Children's wear	1	–	–	1
5651	Family clothes	1	3	–	4
5662	Men's shoes	1	1	1	3
5663	Women's shoes	–	1	–	1
5665	Family shoes	1	2	–	3
5712	Furniture	1	1	–	2
5714	Drapery	1	–	–	1
5732	Radio & T.V.	1	1	–	2
5733	Music stores	–	1	–	1
5812	Eating places	7	4	7	18
5813	Bars	1	3	12	16
5912	Drug stores	3	2	1	6
5921	Liquor stores	1	1	1	3

TABLE 21 - Continued

S.I.C. Code	Description	Frequency			
		(1)	(2)	(3)	(4)
5934	Secondhand furniture	–	1	–	1
5939	Secondhand stores not elsewhere classified	–	–	3	3
5971	Jewelry stores	1	2	1	4
5993	Cigar stores	–	–	1	1
5997	Gift & novelty	1	–	–	1
5999	Miscellaneous retail	–	1	1	2
60	Banks	–	1	1	2
605	Currency exchange	1	2	–	3
6159	Loans (personal)	–	1	–	1
65	Real estate agents	1	–	1	2
7211	Dry cleaners	3	–	–	3
7215	Laundromats	1	2	–	3
7241	Barbers	1	2	4	7
7251	Shoe repairs	–	–	2	2
7631	Watch repairs	–	1	–	1
783	Motion picture theaters	1	2	2	5
801	Medical services	–	–	1	1
8099	Optometrist	1	–	–	1
Vacant		1	2	6	9

Notes: (1) North and California
(2) Madison and Western
(3) Madison and Halsted
(4) Total number of establishments of each function in the sample centers.

TABLE 22

THE FUNCTIONAL STRUCTURE OF WORKINGMEN'S MAJOR SAMPLE CENTERS

S.I.C. Code	Description	Frequency			
		(1)	(2)	(3)	(4)
5231	Paint & glass	–	2	–	2
5251	Hardware	1	2	–	3
5311	Department stores	1	2	1	4
5331	Variety	4	4	2	10
5392	Army & navy	2	2	–	4
5411	Grocery	–	1	9	10
5422	Meat markets	1	5	–	6
5423	Fish	–	–	2	2
5441	Candy	4	3	–	7
5462	Bakeries	1	2	–	3
5612	Men's & boys' clothes	11	6	12	29
5621	Women's clothes	15	10	8	33
5631	Millinery	2	2	3	7
5632	Lingerie	3	–	–	3
5633	Hosiery	1	–	–	1
5634	Apparel accessory	1	–	–	1
5641	Children's wear	–	2	2	4
5651	Family clothes	–	–	3	3
5662	Men's shoes	5	7	–	12
5663	Women's shoes	5	–	1	6
5665	Family shoes	7	6	8	21
5681	Furriers	–	1	–	1
5712	Furniture	3	5	4	12
6713	Floor covering	–	2	–	2
5714	Drapery	2	2	1	5
5719	Miscellaneous furnishings	–	1	1	2
5722	Appliances	4	1	2	7
5732	Radio & T.V.	–	–	1	1
5733	Music stores	–	1	2	3

TABLE 22 – Continued

S.I.C. Code	Description	Frequency			
		(1)	(2)	(3)	(4)
5812	Eating places	7	8	6	21
5813	Bars	3	–	3	6
5912	Drug stores	2	3	2	7
5921	Liquor stores	–	–	1	1
5943	Stationery	–	1	–	1
5952	Sporting goods	–	1	–	1
5971	Jewelry stores	5	4	4	13
5993	Cigar stores	–	1	1	2
5997	Gift & novelty	1	1	3	5
5999	Miscellaneous retail	1	1	–	2
60	Banks	1	1	1	3
6159	Loans (personal)	2	2	–	4
7211	Dry cleaners	–	2	–	2
7221	Photographers	–	1	–	1
7231	Beauty shops	1	–	–	1
7241	Barbers	1	–	1	2
783	Motion picture theaters	1	2	–	3
801	Medical services	1	–	–	1
8099	Optometrists	2	3	1	6
Vacant		4	18	5	27

Notes: (1) Madison and Pulaski
(2) 111th and Michigan
(3) Roosevelt and Halsted
(4) Total number of establishments of each function in sample centers.

Secondhand stores are, however, not characteristic, but army and navy stores offering cheap kinds of clothing items are well represented. The centers are, in general, characterized by a greater range of goods and services offered, especially in the clothing and furniture lines, but lack the more specialized functions typical of the regional centers in the Rest of the City.

Table 16 shows the proportion of establishments in the S. I. C. major groups at minor and major centers. The table reveals interesting differences between the two groups of centers. Outstanding is the very high degree of concentration of establishments in the eating and drinking group (58), accounting for 23.2 percent in minor centers, but only 8.4 percent in major centers. Minor centers are quite similar to neighborhood centers in this respect. Minor centers also have a greater proportion of establishments in the miscellaneous group (59), 14.3 percent compared to 10.0 percent in major centers; in personal services (72) with 10.2 percent of establishments compared to 1.8 percent in major centers; and are also typified by a larger proportion of other central functions not classified into groups, for example real estate agents and banking functions.

On the other hand, the higher proportion of establishments in the clothing group (56) in the major centers, where they occupy 38.0 percent, differentiates them from the minor centers with only 16.0 percent in this group. Major centers also have a higher proportion of establishments in the furniture group (57). In these centers the latter account for 10.0 percent compared to only 4.0 percent in the minor centers. There is also a marked increase in the proportion of stores in the variety group (53), accounting for 5.5 percent compared to only 1.3 percent in minor centers. On the other hand, the two groups of centers are roughly the same in the proportion of establishments in the food group (54).

A Comparison between Nucleations in the Workingmen's Area
and in the Rest of the City

Comparative analysis of the individual types and proportions of
establishments by S. I. C. groups reveals interesting similarities in
functional structure between the centers in both areas of the city.
Allowing for differences in thresholds arising from changes in demand,
minor centers appear quite similar to the larger neighborhood/smaller
community level centers. Major centers, on the other hand, are quite
like regional level centers in the Rest of the City. Minor centers are
very similar to neighborhood centers in the proportion of establishments in the food group (54), but are somewhat larger with respect to
the proportion in the clothing group (56), although essentially the same
types of goods are offered from both groups of centers. They are,
however, unique in the high degree of concentration of bars in the city.
The major centers are especially similar to regional centers in the
proportion of establishments in the furniture (57), eating and drinking
(58), and food (54) groups, although the high threshold specialized
functions are lacking.

What appears to have happened is that the major and minor centers
in the Workingmen's Area have declined in relative size without any
fundamental change in their relative functional structure. This is
shown clearly in Figure 11. With respect to number of establishments
and business types, major and minor centers are most similar to the
community and neighborhood centers respectively. However, from the
point of functional structure they appear most similar to the regional
and community centers, respectively.

This throws light on the dynamics of a system of central places
associated with the continual physical, economic and social changes
especially characteristic of the complexly integrated urban scene.

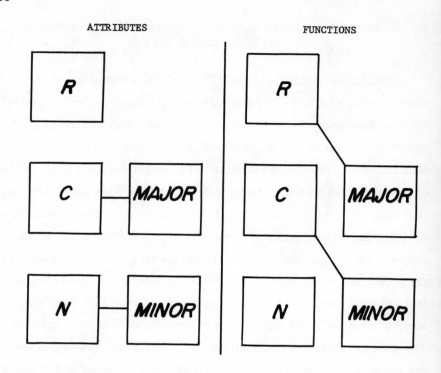

ATTRIBUTES   FUNCTIONS

FIGURE 11: DIAGRAMMATIC REPRESENTATION OF THE SHIFT IN FUNCTIONAL
STRUCTURE OF THE WORKINGMEN'S CENTERS

The marked absence of the more specialized functions in the major centers is presumably related to the loss of thresholds needed for their support. Furthermore, overall reduction in thresholds results in the loss of some establishments which, in turn reduces the degree of duplication. On the other hand, there appears a relatively high degree of duplication of those functions characterized by low thresholds and to which a high proportion of income is directed, for example, food stores and possibly bars. The net result of this process is a shrinkage in the physical size of centers, as indicated by the smaller number of establishments and business types present. The higher number of vacancies in the workingmen's centers, and the increase in non-central functions within the nucleations can also be explained in terms of decline. Although this postulate is not verified by time-series analysis in this work, the argument is consistent with underlying premise of a dynamic central place theory and points out the need for further time-oriented studies.

We can thus consider the major and minor centers in the Workingmen's Area relative to the regional and community level centers in the Rest of the City. The absence of neighborhood equivalents in the low income area can be related to the generally lower level of land values. By using the $750 cutoff point in this work, the smallest nucleations in the Workingmen's Area have not been identified.

Summary of the Characteristics of the Hierarchy
of Retail Nucleations

The increasing functional complexity associated with higher levels in the hierarchy of retail nucleations, and furthermore, the close degree of similarity between major and minor centers and regional and community centers respectively, is clearly illustrated at the third level of aggregation of functions shown in Figure 12. The diagram

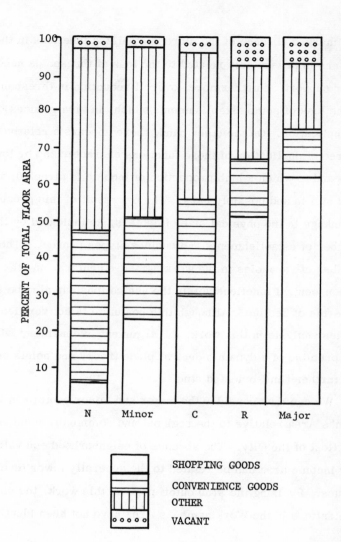

FIGURE 12: THE PROPORTION OF TOTAL FLOOR AREA DEVOTED TO CONVENIENCE, SHOPPING AND OTHER GOODS BY LEVEL OF RETAIL NUCLEATION

shows central functions grouped according to the distinctions used in planning literature between convenience, shopping and other uses. The proportions are based on floor area in this case to take into account changes in the size of nucleations with increasing level in the hierarchy.

The proportion of floor space devoted to convenience goods is directly related to the proportion devoted to other uses, but inversely related to the proportion of floor space devoted to shopping goods.

Further comparison between these aggregated categories and the physical characteristics of centers is illustrated in Figure 13. The proportion of convenience goods decreases with an increase in the number of business types and establishments. This reflects the greater importance attached to higher level centers for multiple purpose shopping goods trips. Although trend lines have only been fitted by eye in the diagrams, they suffice to point out the consistent deviation of the major centers. Major centers are characterized by fewer convenience goods than expected from the number of establishments and business types, and conversely, a much higher proportion of shopping goods. This is in direct support of the argument that they approximate regional centers from the point of functional composition.

From the evidence presented, the viability of the classification of centers into different levels in a hierarchy based upon the analysis of numbers of establishments and business types is supported. The centers at each level appear to differ in functional composition according to the premise of the theory of tertiary activity.

Peak Values and the Hierarchy

In Chapter I, it was argued that stratification of retail nucleations into levels of a hierarchy also implies stratification in general level of land values, and it was argued, in peak values. This is based on the relationship

$$V_{pk} = g \left(\sum_{i=1}^{m} T_i \right) \qquad (1:13)$$

whereby peak land values may be used as an index of the relative importance of retail nucleations, since increased level in the hierarchy
is associated with increased peak values.

Data in general support of this hypothesis are presented in
Table 23. Regional centers are associated with the highest average
peak values, followed by community and neighborhood centers, respectively. In the low income part of the study area, the average peak
value for the major centers is higher than that of the minor centers.
Variance analysis indicates that the mean peak values are significantly
different, as shown in Table 24.

However, further analysis using t-tests of the differences in mean
peak values between individual levels in the hierarchy indicates that
all levels do not differ significantly from each other. Rather, the
overall difference suggested by Table 24 does, in fact, comprise two
groups. These are shown in Table 25. On the one hand, there is no
significant difference between the average peak value of the highest
level centers -- the regional and major centers, respectively. On the
other hand, there does not appear to be a significant difference between
the peak values of the other levels -- the community, neighborhood and
the minor centers, respectively. This is in spite of the differences in
the numbers of business types offered from them. Furthermore, it is
noted that although minor and major centers are most like neighborhood and community level centers in respect to physical attributes,
their peak values tend toward the community and regional levels to
which they are functionally most similar.

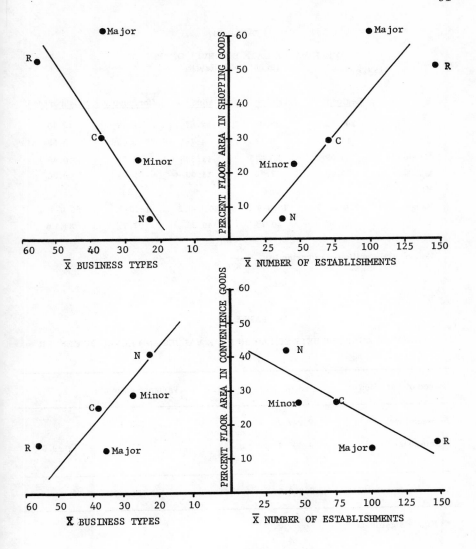

FIGURE 13: SELECTED RELATIONSHIPS BETWEEN FUNCTIONAL STRUCTURE AND
PHYSICAL CHARACTERISTICS IN THE HIERARCHY OF RETAIL NUCLEATIONS

TABLE 23

PEAK VALUE DATA BY LEVEL OF CENTER
(in 00's of dollars)

	Regional	Major	Minor	Community	Neighborhood
s^2	268.82	83.05	22.67	10.17	12.70
s	16.4	9.113	4.761	3.189	3.564
$\overline{X}$ value	29.63	20.375	11.833	11.50	10.45
M_d value	25.00	17.75	11.00	12.0	9.00
N.	11	8	9	23	11
Range	70.0-12.5	40.0-8.5	20.0-8.5	18.0-7.5	20.0-7.5
$V^{(1)}$	55.3%	40.7%	40.2%	27.7%	34.1%

Notes: (1) Coefficient of variability $= \dfrac{s}{\overline{X}}$

TABLE 24

VARIANCE ANALYSIS BETWEEN MEAN PEAK VALUES AND LEVEL OF CENTER

Source of Variation	S.S.	d.f.	Variance estimate	F
Between level	2,942.7	4	735.7	
Within level	4,408.1	57	77.3	9.5**
Total	7,350.8	61	(Foc.01 = 2.53)	

** Highly significant

TABLE 25

DIFFERENCES IN MEAN PEAK LAND VALUE
BETWEEN INDIVIDUAL LEVELS IN THE HIERARCHY OF RETAIL NUCLEATIONS

Level of Center		1	2	3	4	5
Regional	1	X	No	Yes	Yes	Yes
Major	2	No[1]	X	Yes	Yes	Yes
Community	3	Yes	Yes	X	No[2]	No
Neighborhood	4	Yes	Yes	No	X	No[3]
Minor	5	Yes	Yes	No	No	X

Notes: No indicates no significant difference.

Yes indicates significant difference.

(1) computed = 1.36 (.05 = 2.1)

(2) computed = .838 (.05 = 2.04)

(3) Inferred from test between community and neighborhood level, given peak value data in Table 23.

94

There is a marked degree of variation in peak values at centers within any level in the hierarchy. Dispersion is most marked in the higher level centers in both parts of the study area. Absolute dispersion cannot be meaningfully measured, however, without reference to the average about which it occurs. Relative dispersion of peak values within any level of the hierarchy, measured by the coefficient of variability, is shown in Table 23. Peak values show the largest relative within group dispersion at regional centers. Peak values in the two groups of centers in the Workingmen's Area vary to about the same degree, but much less than the regional centers. Community level centers exhibit the least amount of variation in peak values.

Peak values at the centers of one level tend to overlap with similar values at different levels in the hierarchy. This is shown in Figure 14, which suggests that the relationship (1:13) above is perhaps an over-simplification of the real world situation. Part of the variation in peak values can be associated with the general decline in land values away from the center of the city where they are at zenith. Variation is to be expected since centers at any level are located at varying distances from the city center. Further explanation is probably found in the notion of a lag in land values associated with the decline of centers, especially in blighted areas. Mayer points out that "...land values do not immediately react to change in conditions affecting the business areas; there is usually a lag of a year or two."[9]

The idea of a lag in values offers attractive possibilities for explaining the situation in the Workingmen's centers. Both the major and minor centers have higher peak values than are expected from the number of business types offered. According to Mayer, "...the centers in the near blighted and blighted areas, with but few exceptions,

[9] H. M. Mayer, "Patterns and Recent Trends...," op. cit., p. 4.

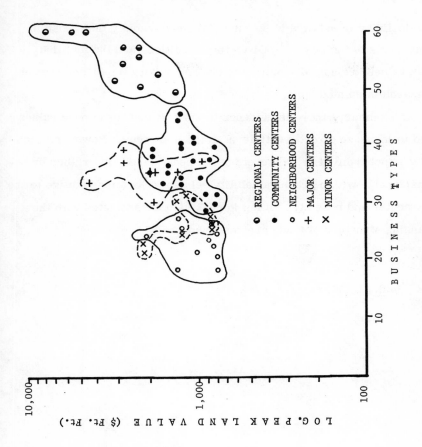

FIGURE 14: THE RELATIONSHIP BETWEEN PEAK LAND VALUE AND NUMBER OF BUSINESS TYPES
BY LEVEL OF RETAIL NUCLEATION, CITY OF CHICAGO, 1961

are declining in relative importance far more rapidly than those in other parts of the city."[10] Given this condition, and the fact that peak values are not so sensitive to change, a very important area of research is pointed up.

In summary, there is evidence to suggest that mean peak values tend to increase directly with level in the hierarchy. However, each level is not typified by a discrete set of peak values, but rather by considerable within group variability related to location relative to the city center and possibly to a lag in peak values associated with the changing structure of trade areas served.

[10] Ibid., p. 14.

CHAPTER IV

THE INTERNAL STRUCTURE OF RETAIL NUCLEATIONS

It has been observed that there is an essential order to the land use pattern.[1] This takes the form of specialization of activities in space. Ratcliff argues that the regularity of land use patterns results from the underlying causes of urbanization itself. Since these are basically economic, he argues that the arrangement of land uses within any area is an extension of the economic forces. He states, "...the locational pattern of land use in urban areas results from basic economic forces, and the arrangement of activities at strategic points on

---

[1]Examples of this order are expressed in the concentric zone theory, sector theory and multiple nucleii theory of urban form, for which see respectively, E. W. Burgess, "The Growth of the City," in The City , ed. R. E. Park, E. W. Burgess and R. D. McKenzie (Chicago: University of Chicago Press, 1925), pp. 47-62; H. Hoyt, "City Growth and Mortgage Risk," Insured Mortgage Portfolio, 1 (1936-37), passim, and idem , The Structure and Growth of Residential Neighborhoods in American Cities , (Washington, D.C.: Government Printing Office, 1939); C. D. Harris and E. L. Ullman, "The Nature of Cities," Annals of the American Academy of Political and Social Science , CCXLII (1945), pp. 7-17.

the web of transportation lines is a part of the economic process of society."[2]

The basic elements of this process can be summarized as follows:

1. Each activity has the ability to derive utility from every piece of land. The utility is measured by the rent the activity is willing, and able, to pay for the land.

2. Therefore, the greater the derivable utility, the greater the rent an activity is willing to pay for the use of the land.

3. Competition in the urban land market results, in the long run, in an equilibrium pattern of land uses in which each site is occupied by the "highest and best" uses. This is the one that can derive the greatest utility from the site, and, therefore, is willing to pay the most for its use.

4. As a result of this process, rents throughout the system are maximized.

The result of this process is an orderly arrangement of land uses. Traditionally, this has been viewed at a highly aggregative level through the identification of major areas of similar land use within the urban area as a whole. Thus, for example, the pattern of concentric zones of different land uses proposed by Burgess can be explained in this way. There is no reason, however, why the basic process should not be extended to include micro-patterns in the arrangement of land uses within retail nucleations.

Site Utility and Retailing

The utility that is added to a site over and above the capital and labor applied to it is essentially that added by its location. In a

[2]R. U. Ratcliff, Urban Land Economics, op. cit., p. 46.

retailing framework, location is viewed as the accessibility or centrality afforded by a particular site to a portion of the urban market.
Centrality may be viewed at two levels; (a) the macro-level, or
differences in accessibility between alternate business centers, and
(b) the micro-level, or the differences in advantage of site to local
concentrations of consumers within the different levels of retail nucleation.

The fundamental importance of centrality at the broader level has
been discussed above as the underlying reasons for the specific location of individual centers comprising the hierarchy. Centrality at the
more refined level is measured relative to local concentrations of
shoppers at sites within any retail nucleation. Presumably, the higher
the level of center in the hierarchy, the greater the local concentration
of shoppers. Since retail nucleations are areas of retail land use
rather than simply points in space, there is not only variation in the
concentration of shoppers between alternate centers, but also between
alternative locations within any level of center. Specifically, there is
a decline in the concentration of shoppers as distance away from the
peak intersection increases.

Another aspect of site utility concerned with locations within
business centers is related to the proximity of a particular business
type to complementary uses in the center. Presumably each type
seeks a different set of relationships with other businesses depending
upon the "bundle of goods" offered and the buying habits associated
with them. In this way, some retail businesses are complementary
to each other, whilst others are non-complementary. In general, the
most desirable relationship is one that maximizes the sharing of
clientele with adjacent uses.[3]

[3]Some examples of these functional associations are presented in

Rent and Site Utility

To secure the locational advantage offered by a particular site within a business center, an activity must pay certain costs. This largely takes the form of rents -- the charge made by landowners for the use of their sites. Rent is therefore an opportunity cost which must be paid by a business to obtain site utility. From the argument above, the higher the site utility for a specific use, the greater the rent which has to be paid. This notion was voiced early by Hurd, who states that, "...in cities, economic rent is based on superiority of location only - the sole function of urban land being to furnish area on which to erect buildings."[4] More recently, Chamberlin argued, "...the rent of urban land is explained wholly...by the factor of location.[5]

However, it is possible for factors other than location to influence competitive bidding for site utility, and thereby affect the level of rent and land values. These factors included, on the one hand, site, shape, size, topography and geology, and on the other, accessibility to other physical factors in the system, such as sewers, street lighting, etc.. More important, however, from the retailing viewpoint, is the "physical quality" of site.

---

[3] R. E. Murphy, J. E. Vance, and J. Epstein, "Internal Structure of the C. B. D.," Economic Geography, 31 (1955), pp. 21-46.

[4] R. M. Hurd, Principles of City Land Values, The Record and Guide, (New York, 1924), p. 26.

[5] E. H. Chamberlin, The Theory of Monopolistic Competition, (Cambridge, Mass.: Harvard University Press, seventh edition, 1960), p. 266.

The "physical quality" of a site in this context refers to the "fixity of investment," the capital committed in the form of buildings. Until such development, site productivity is variable, and is fixed predominantly by external factors, principally location. Once developed, however, site productivity is relatively fixed and permanent, and subject to _internal_ site variation. The latter is in the form of the buildings committed on the site. Although this is important in some cases in determining values, it must be considered secondary to location. Buildings can often be easily remodelled to suit new tenants, since the production aspect of retailing does not differ greatly between activities.

Evidence that the "fixity of investment" does act as a constraining influence, and that pre-existing store structures cannot always be remodelled to suit new tenants is reflected in the notion of _functional_ _blight_. Functional blight results when sites and buildings are no longer adequate for efficient retailing operation. This factor has been emphasized in recent years by the attention given to it by planners. Recent changes in the technology of retailing, especially those associated with increased scale of operation, including the need for parking space, have accentuated the constraints imposed by the "fixity of investment," and have in part given rise to the marked increase in the "freestanding" element of the retail structure discussed above.

It is the locational aspects of rent that are important here. In this context rents are considered by Ratcliff as a levy imposed by landlords as a substitute for savings in consumer transfer costs.[6] Transfer costs are not physical but economic. They represent convenience with a dollar sign. Functional connections with other

---

[6]R. U. Ratcliff, "The Dynamics of Efficiency...,"_op. cit._, 302-3.

points in space are essential to the life of the retailing establishment. Although they vary naturally between activities, a cost factor is always involved. In retailing activities, such costs are primarily those of moving people and goods between home bases and business centers. Locations are thus sought which minimize costs of consumer movement. It was pointed out above how fundamental this is in the satisfaction of individual firm thresholds.

The substitution of rent for consumer transfer costs was the fundamental hypothesis in the early writings of Haig. He states,

> 'Rent appears as the charge which the owner of a relatively accessible site can impose because of the savings in transportation cost which the use of his site makes possible. The activities which can stand high rents are those where large savings in transport costs may be realized by locating on central sites where accessibility is greatest."[7]

Chamberlin opposes this viewpoint and considers that, "Rents are not paid in order to save transportation charges. It is paid in order to secure a larger volume of sales."[8] Such a difference would appear to be in kind only, since the amount a producer can sell is restricted by location. If not, department stores would locate in outlying districts, secure larger or the same volume of sales, but increase profits from savings in rents. The reason why this does not occur is presumably because sales are greatest at those points which minimize the distance to the portion of the urban market served, and thus the firm is substituting rents for consumer costs and at the same time is paying directly for added sales volume.

[7] R. M. Haig, "Major Factors...," op. cit., p. 87.

[8] E. H. Chamberlin, op. cit., p. 267.

Although Chamberlin's argument is applicable to the differences in rent between alternate retail nucleations, it has greater relevance than Haig's to the location of businesses within any given retail nucleation. The principle cost to the consumer is that involved in making the shopping trip from the home-base to the business center itself. However, once the consumer has arrived at the center, it would appear that the costs involved are basically time-costs which stem from the purpose underlying the trip. Since retail nucleations generally do not extend for more than two blocks either side of the peak intersection, and in most cases are much smaller in extent than this, it is difficult to perceive how internal rent variation can be explained by Haig's thesis.

Rather, the notion of rent as a payment for added sales volume would appear as a more meaningful explanation of differences in rents within retail nucleations. Getis has demonstrated that total sales volume decreases with increased distance from the peak intersection.[9] Thus, within retail nucleations:

$$\text{Sales} = f \text{ (distance)} \qquad (4:1)$$

Presumably the basis for this relationship is that the local concentration of shoppers within the nucleation is also directly related to distance from the peak intersection where it is at its peak concentration,[10]

$$\text{Buyers} = g \text{ (distance)} \qquad (4:2)$$

and therefore,

$$\text{Sales} = h \text{ (buyers)} \qquad (4:3)$$

[9] A. Getis, "A Theoretical and Empirical Inquiry into the Spatial Structure of Retail Activities," (unpublished Ph.D. dissertation, University of Washington, Seattle, 1961).

[10] Graphs in support of this are included in B. J. L. Berry and H. M. Mayer, Comparative Studies ..., op. cit.

Moreover, analysis of the land value surface within any retail nucleation clearly indicates the decline in value, and therefore rent, as distance from the peak lot increases. Thus,

$$\text{Rent} = f \text{ (distance)} \qquad (4:4)$$

It follows from the relationships presented above, that,

$$\text{Rent} = f \text{ (sales)} = g \text{ (buyers)} \qquad (4:5)$$

The two viewpoints are wedded in the above fashion, therefore. The rent at any site can perhaps be considered theoretically as comprising two parts. On the one hand, there is a general level of rent associated with the different levels of business centers in the hierarchy, which is related to savings in transport costs resulting from the degree of centrality enjoyed by the center relative to the portion of the urban market it services. On the other hand, there are variations in rent over and above the general level within any given nucleation resulting from locational advantages of individual sites with respect to local concentrations of shoppers and, hence, to sales volume.

Thresholds and Rents

Threshold has been defined as the minimum sales volume required for the initial operation or the condition of entry of any retail business type. Furthermore, it has been pointed out that all business types are ordered according to threshold size. Since sales volume and rents are related in (4:5) above, it follows that a relationship should also exist between thresholds and rents.

Imagine a regional level nucleation. Sales volumes will decline with distance away from the peak intersection in that center, as shown by line SR in Figure 15. Each business type can be located along line SR at distances from the peak intersection where threshold sales are just satisfied. Three business types, A, B and C, are located at threshold on the curve.

From the arguments presented above, however, lower level nucleations will be associated with lower sales volumes. This is shown in Figure 16 in which lines SR, SC, and SN represent total sales volumes within regional, community and neighborhood centers respectively. Threshold sales for all three types are satisfied on curve SR. However, on curve SC, threshold levels are satisfied only for types B and C. Because of this, type A will not be represented. By the same argument, threshold for type C only is satisfied on curve SN, and neither types A nor B will be represented. Types B and C are examples of hierarchical marginal goods referred to above. This pattern in the allocation of business types is consistent with the premises of the hierarchy of retail nucleations presented above.

From relationship (4:4), and from the relationship in Figure 15,

$$\text{Threshold} = f \text{ (distance)} \qquad (4:6)$$

it follows that,

$$\text{Rents} = g \text{ (threshold sales)} \qquad (4:7)$$

This relationship is shown in graphical form in Figure 17. Thus, it is hypothesized that high rent paying functions will be at the same time high threshold functions.

An interesting feature emerges from closer inspection of Figure 16. It is apparent that something can now be said about the location of business types within any retail nucleation once threshold sizes are known. For example, the threshold for business type A is satisfied on curve SR only within distance VO from the peak intersection, V. It is impossible for type A to locate at distances greater than VO from the peak of a regional center, or appear at distance VO in either community (curve SC) or neighborhood (curve SN) centers, since sales volume is not high enough to satisfy its threshold. In a similar

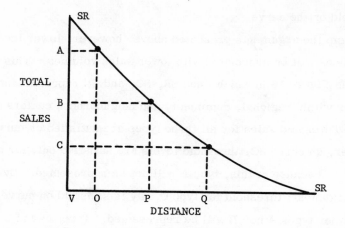

FIGURE 15: IDEAL RELATIONSHIP BETWEEN SALES AND DISTANCE FROM PEAK
INTERSECTION AT A REGIONAL CENTER

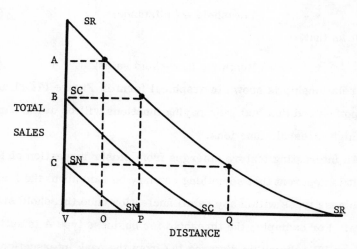

FIGURE 16: IDEAL RELATIONSHIP BETWEEN SALES AND DISTANCE FROM PEAK
INTERSECTION AT DIFFERENT LEVELS IN A HIERARCHY

way, type B cannot locate at a distance greater than VP from the peak intersection in a regional center (curve SR); can appear only at V, the peak intersection itself, in a community center; and will not appear at all in neighborhood centers. The same argument can be extended to account for the location of type C within the regional, community and neighborhood centers. Hence, the arrangement of functions within a retail nucleation can be described on the basis of thresholds. Thus, within a retail nucleation possessing the sales curve SR, as shown in Figure 16, VO, VP and VQ can be termed the threshold distances for business types A, B and C respectively. Accordingly, each business type occupies a specific point location within the center.

A Simple Spatial Model

A simple spatial model to illustrate the ordered pattern of the arrangement of functions within retail nucleations may be derived from an adaptation of the discussion by Isard.[11] In this case, site utility, represented by volume of sales, varies directly with distance (from 4:1 above); costs of the individual business types vary with threshold. Given these conditions, a concentric-circle pattern of retail land use results within any nucleation. Rents are maximized, with every site occupied by the "highest and best" use according to the underlying process of development.

Figure 18 illustrates hypothetical rent gradients based on the cost structures of activities A and B. If the cost structure of activity A is such that sheer volume of sales is associated with rapidly increasing profits, (for example, if fixed costs are an important part of total

[11]W. Isard, Location and Space Economy, (New York: Wiley and Sons Inc., 1956), pp. 200-206.

108

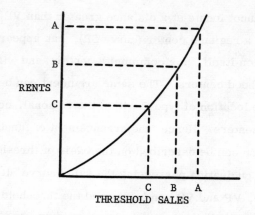

FIGURE 17: THE RELATIONSHIP BETWEEN RENTS AND THRESHOLD SALES

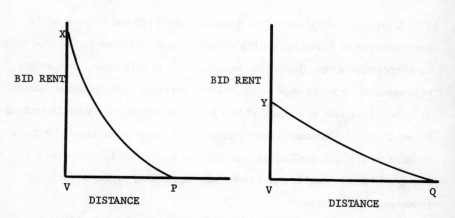

FIGURE 18: HYPOTHETICAL RENT GRADIENTS FOR TWO BUSINESS TYPES

costs), then the amount of rent which can be paid will increase rapidly with sales volumes. If we assume that sales volume is just large enough to permit normal profits at P, this will become the threshold distance for that activity provided that there are no competitive uses. When the high sales volumes at the peak intersection, V, are enjoyed, activity A will receive enough in the way of Profits to afford rent VX.

In the case of activity B, the critical difference is in the slope of the rent gradient which reflects a lesser sensitivity of profits to total revenue. Since it takes less total sales for activity B to earn normal profits, Q becomes the threshold distance when there is no competition from alternative uses. However, the volume of sales which gave activity A enough profits to pay rent VX at V will give activity B only enough to pay rent VY. This situation would arise if variable costs for activity B associated with increased volume of sales increased at a much greater rate than fixed costs.

Figure 19 shows the rent gradients for activities A, B, and C in competition with each other for sites in the retail nucleation. Once competition is introduced, it is immediately apparent that the freedom to locate is restricted for each of the three types. In the non-competitive system, types A, B and C were able to appear anywhere between VO, VP and VQ respectively. However, in competition, activity A, for example, experiences a more rapid increase in profits with distance than activity B. But profits for A are large enough for it to pay a higher rent than activity B only at T. Similarly, profits for activity B, which increase more rapidly than those of activity C, enable it to pay a higher rent than C at R. If the above is true, then the threshold would seem to be competitive when equated to the possibilities of achieving scale economies by which average costs are reduced. Supra-normal profits would only be earned when the cost structure of any given activity is such that variable costs increase much less

110

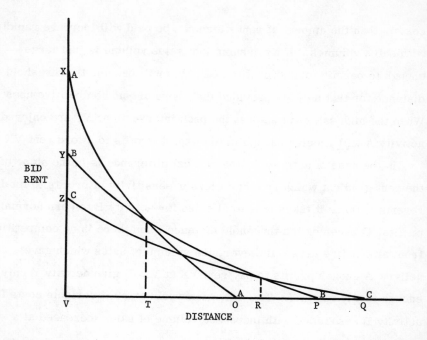

FIGURE 19: TYPICAL RENT GRADIENTS FOR REGIONAL, COMMUNITY AND NEIGHBORHOOD
LEVEL BUSINESS TYPES

rapidly than fixed costs. If, on the other hand, all excess profits are bid away as rent, each activity will only earn normal profits at any point on its sales curve.

Under the above conditions, activity A will be able to afford higher rents and outbid the other activities for all sites from V, the peak intersection, to T; similarly, from T to R, activity B will occupy sites; and from R to Q, activity C will be the successful competitor. Generalization of the system from two to three dimensions by the rotation of VQ about V yields an optimum concentric circle pattern of functional arrangement within the retail nucleation in which the "highest and best use" occupies each site.

Thus far, we have been dealing with only three types of retail businesses, A, B and C. These can be imagined as representatives of the regional, community and neighborhood types respectively. However, at each level in the hierarchy there is a set of business types, not simply one type. Furthermore, as the model stands, an assumption made above is openly violated. In Figure 19, types A, B and C are able to occupy zones, whereas the assumption is that all types shall occupy point locations. To overcome this apparent incongruity, and to take cognizance of a set of activities at each level, line AA must be considered as some combination of the rent gradients of all the regional business types; line BB as a combination of the set of community level functions; and line CC similarly derived for the set of neighborhood functions. Thus, within distance VT from the peak intersection, sites will be occupied by regional functions, and between TR and RQ sites will be occupied by community and neighborhood functions respectively.

Higher level business types will be absent from lower level centers. In Figure 20 the system is extended to include lower level centers. At the community level, regional level business types will not appear on

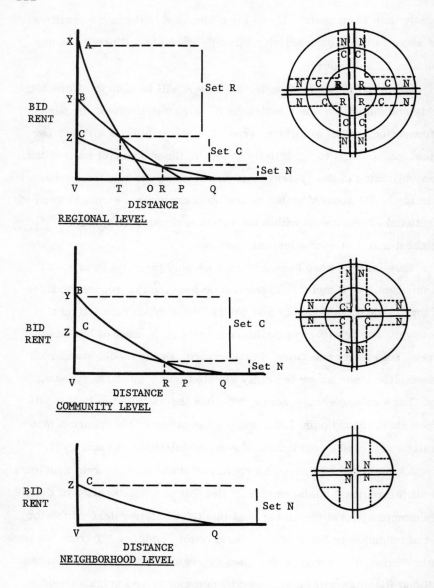

FIGURE 20: HYPOTHETICAL INTERNAL STRUCTURE OF REGIONAL, COMMUNITY AND
NEIGHBORHOOD LEVEL RETAIL NUCLEATIONS

account of the lower-than-threshold sales volumes. Thus, community level activities (set BB above) will occupy the core area VR and these will be surrounded concentrically by neighborhood level types, which occupy RQ. In the neighborhood level centers, only the set of neighborhood functions (set CC above) will appear, and they will consequently occupy the entire business center.

It is now possible to present a generalized structure of any business center. Theoretically, under the assumptions of the simple model, the internal arrangement of retail uses is as follows:

(1) The threshold size continuum is expressed spatially such that the highest threshold activity is closer to the peak than all others and consequently, occupies the highest value land. It will be surrounded concentrically by other business types in order of decreasing threshold size.

(2) The core area of any retail nucleation will be occupied by that group of functions that differentiates the center from the preceding lower level in the hierarchy.

(3) Because lower level functions are displaced outwards at each succeeding higher level in the hierarchy, they will occur on lower value land as order in the hierarchy increases.

(4) Within the group of functions typical of any given level in the hierarchy, each business type will be located according to its position along the threshold size continuum, similar to the arrangement in (1) above. Thus the highest threshold neighborhood type will, for example, occupy the highest value land of all the other neighborhood types, etc. .

More Complex Models

In the real world, the arrangement of retail uses within any retail nucleation, does not conform to such a rigid geometrical pattern as envisaged in the simple model presented above. A cursory inspection

of any business center indicates that the arrangement of retailing
activities is much more complex, and in fact at first glance does not
appear to conform to any pattern whatsoever. Establishments of a
given type are not clearly associated with discrete "economic distances"
from the peak intersection. Rather, there is considerable variability
in their location with respect to the peak intersection.[12] Consequently,
all establishments of a given business type do not occupy the same
value land, and presumably therefore, they do not all have the same
rent paying ability. The location of retail activities is considerably
less deterministic than the model implies, and real world patterns are
as a result considerably more complex.

However, more complex patterns do not necessarily imply that
underlying structure or order in land use patterns is absent in the real
world. This is nicely illustrated by Dunn, who referring to the
parallel case of agricultural land use patterns, notes that when com-
plicating factors are applied to the simple concentric pattern envisaged
by von Thunen,

> "The simplicity of land use patterns is destroyed
> once and for all. However, this does not mean
> that the order and system are destroyed. It means
> that the order imposed by the influence of economic
> distance takes on increasingly more complex forms
> ...."[13]

It is apparent, therefore, that although the assumptions upon
which the simple model are based may not be invalid, they are in need
of modification to take into account the increasingly more complex
order imposed by the influence of economic distance. Especially,

---

[12] For empirical illustration of this see B. J. Garner, "Land
Values ...," op. cit.

[13] E. S. Dunn, Jr., The Location of Agricultural Production,
(Gainesville, Fla.: University of Florida Press, 1954), p. 61.

they need to be relaxed to take into account the extreme variability in location exhibited by establishments of any particular business type.

Product Differentiation

The rigid geometrical pattern envisaged by the simple model is based upon the explicit assumption that each business type is associated with a discrete but different threshold sales value. Moreover, by implication, all establishments of a given business type were considered to operate at the same threshold level.

Thus, all establishments of a given business type are presumed to be offering identical goods from identical stores. It follows also that they are therefore serving an identical or homogeneous urban market. These conditions are, of course, the underlying assumptions of pure competition, which was one of the basic assumptions of the simple model.

The urban market, as pointed out above, does not comprise a simple set of consumer demands. Rather, it consists of a complex pattern of different tastes, needs and preferences which stem directly from the differences in available amounts of disposable income. In this sense it can be considered as being comprised of a series of different levels, or strata, within which each consumer is located according to his income, social and ethnic characteristics. Furthermore, the urban market becomes more complex because any consumer can shop at a higher level or lower level in the urban market depending upon which needs are being satisfied.

It would seem reasonable, therefore, to hypothesize that establishments of a given business type do not offer identical goods from identical stores, and that consumers are not paired with just any seller. More realistically, consumers are linked to particular establishments for the purchase of a given good according to their preferences and position in the various strata of the urban market.

Take, for example, the case of bars within any retail nucleation. Their character may range from the chic cocktail lounge all the way to the perfectly dismal "joint." When the urban market is viewed as comprising a variety of different levels of consumer demands, the differences between various bars would presumably be related to the level of consumer preference serviced. Rather than grouping all bars into one class of business type under the available systems of classification, it would be more realistic to consider them as offering different goods and consequently comprising different business types. A similar argument can be extended to include the classification of all other business types in the retail nucleation. Consequently, we are dealing with not establishments of a variety of different business types, but a large set of establishments each of which constitutes an individual type in itself.

However, it is apparent that there is more than one establishment of a given type which aims to satisfy similar levels of consumer preference. Using the example of bars, there may be a variety of cocktail lounges, and most certainly a wide range of "joints" within a large retail nucleation. Competition between establishments of roughly similar character will be acute as each seeks to attract consumers from that stratum of the market they service.

Establishments are not exactly similar but are differentiated from each other in many subtle ways. Qualitative differences, whether real or fancied in the eyes of the consumer, arise from a combination of (a) differences in the product sold, and (b) differences in the condition surrounding its sale. A variety of factors can bring about the former. These include patents, trade marks, "snob appeal," peculiarities of packaging and singularity of product, design, color and style.

Differences arising out of the character of the conditions surrounding the sale of the good include, according to Chamberlin, primarily that of location of the establishment.[14] It also includes other features such as the general tone of the store, the seller's way of doing business, his reputation for fair dealing and efficiency, and a host of other factors of a personal nature which attach consumers to his particular store rather than to some other. Insofar as these intangibles vary between sellers, they can be viewed as being purchased along with the good in question, since the product in each case is different in the eyes of the buyer. More often than not, the purchase of these intangibles is reflected in an increase in price of the good.

The important aspect of product differentiation for this work is the assumption that there is a different cost structure associated with the unique characteristics of a particular establishment of any given business type. Differences in costs of advertising, size of stock carried, number of employees and other variables is reflected in differences in the relative size and importance of variable to total costs. Consequently, it is realistic to assume that, because of this, there is variation in sales level, and thus profits needed to satisfy threshold.

Modification of the Threshold

Assuming that there are differences in store character and in the proportion of variable costs to the total cost structure of establishments within any given business type, it would appear that the notion of threshold used in the simple model needs to be modified. Thus far, the discussion of thresholds has centered on the differences between

[14] E. H. Chamberlin, op. cit., pp. 56-70.

individual business types. Business types were considered lying along a continuum of threshold size, and all establishments within a given business type were assumed to operate at identical threshold levels. In a competitive system, the actual threshold was determined according to the rent-paying ability of different business types. The arrangement of three business types along such a threshold continuum is illustrated in Figure 21 (A). Business types A, B and C can be considered as typical elements of the set of regional, community and neighborhood functions respectively.

Once the assumption of homogeneity of establishments within any business type is relaxed to include the notion of product differentiation, it is apparent that a simple ranking of business types by threshold size is no longer possible. For any given business type, each establishment will be associated with a different threshold level. Thus, in the case of bars, the chic cocktail bar will have a higher threshold than the "joint." Similarly, a variety of threshold sizes will exist for all other bars between these two limits. A similar variety in thresholds will exist for all establishments of every other business type.

As a result, each business type will be associated with a range of thresholds rather than just a unique threshold size as implied in the operational definitions of threshold used in the current literature.[15] Presumably, the range over which thresholds for each business type vary will be directly related to the degree of product differentiation and the various levels of the urban market served by establishments of that business type. The idea of a range of thresholds for businesses A, B and C is illustrated in Figure 21 (B).

[15]B. J. L. Berry and W. L. Garrison, "The Functional Bases of the Central Place Hierarchy," Economic Geography, 34 (1958), pp. 145-154.

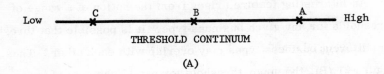

THRESHOLD CONTINUUM

(A)

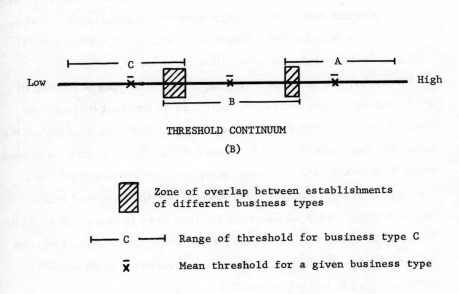

THRESHOLD CONTINUUM

(B)

⬛ (hatched) Zone of overlap between establishments of different business types

├─ C ─┤ Range of threshold for business type C

x̄ Mean threshold for a given business type

FIGURE 21: THE THRESHOLD CONTINUUM SHOWING OVERLAP IN THRESHOLDS FOR DIFFERENT BUSINESS TYPES

An interesting feature arises from the notion of a range of thresholds for any given business type. It is possible that thresholds for different business types may overlap with each other. Thus, in Figure 21 (B), the upper threshold for establishments of business type C overlap with the lower thresholds for establishments of business type B. Similar overlapping occurs between business types B and A. It is therefore possible for thresholds of establishments for several different business types to approximate each other.

However, the notion of a ranking of business types according to threshold size is not destroyed. Although we find that there are as many thresholds for a given business type as there are establishments of it, and that there is overlap between them, they may still be ranked along a threshold size continuum when the mean threshold for each business type is considered. We suggest that the threshold ranking of business types so far alluded to in the literature is really one which is based on the mean threshold size for each type, since there has been no consideration of "within business type" variation in thresholds arising from product differentiation.

A More Complex Model

The introduction of a threshold range for any given business type resulting from differences in cost structures of establishments due to product differentiation, enables modification of the simple model so that it approximates more closely conditions in the real world. Concentric zones of retail land use may still result, but are modified by the competition between establishments of different business types for locations within certain parts of the retail nucleation. In this way, the rigid geometrics of the simple model are relaxed, and more complex, less rigid, patterns are substituted which at the same time do not destroy the underlying order in the system.

Instead of having one threshold for a given business type, we now have many. In effect, there will be one for each establishment. Consequently, the argument presented above by which profits and volume of sales determined rent paying ability applies here not to different business types but to different establishments of the same business type. Since rent paying ability varies for each establishment of a given business type, each activity will, therefore, be characterized by a whole family of differently sloped rent gradients rather than by a single one. Moreover, when the rent gradient of an establishment for one business type approximates that of an establishment for another business type, they can be assumed to be able to offer virtually identical rent-bids for site utility. In this way competition is possible between representatives of different business types for sites at varying distances from the peak intersection.

Figure 22 shows the rent gradients for three business types, A, B and C. Assuming for the moment that only three retail uses are in competition for sites, an optimal pattern of land use results, and the "highest and best" use occupies each site within the nucleation. However, the resultant pattern is much less rigid than that shown in Figure 19 since there are zones of overlap between different uses.

If the rent gradients illustrated by curves AA, BB and CC in the figure are considered to be representative of regional, community and neighborhood level businesses respectively, then Figure 22 shows the pattern of arrangement within a typical regional level nucleation. Activity A will outbid all other types within distance VP; business type B will win out in area OS and similarly, business type C will occupy area RT. Because of the overlapping of thresholds allowed under the assumption of ranges of thresholds for each type, the rent gradients for any two businesses may coincide at certain distances

122

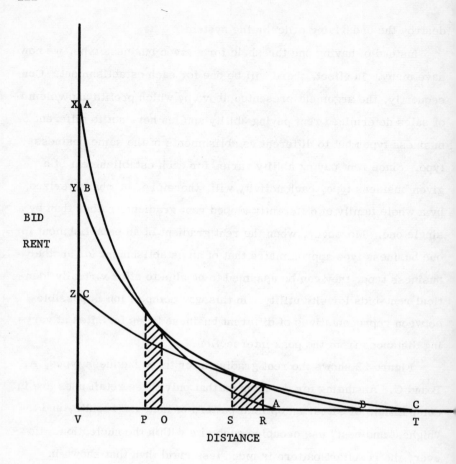

FIGURE 22: HYPOTHETICAL RENT GRADIENTS FOR PRODUCT DIFFERENTIATED
BUSINESS TYPES

from the peak intersection. Thus, within the distance PO and distance SR there will be competition between establishments of different business types for site utility; in the former area, establishments of types A and B will be found, whereas in the latter, establishments of types B and C will be present.

Generalization of the system from two to three dimensions by the rotation of VT about V yields a theoretical pattern in the internal arrangement of functions similar to that illustrated in Figure 23. Extension of the argument and illustration to include many business types at the regional, community and neighborhood levels, and also to include competition between many establishments of a given business type would, it is believed, enable a pattern similar to the real world conditions to be derived.

Moreover, a range of thresholds for any given business type offers a possible explanation for the occurrence of high order business types at lower level centers in the hierarchy. For example, although a particular business type may be classified as a regional level function, if a particular establishment of that type is operating at the lower limit of the range of thresholds, it may be possible for it to secure enough sales and offer high enough rent bids to exist outside of a regional center in, say, a community level center. Although this is not considered typical, it offers an explanation for the apparent lack of rigidity in the allocation of functions to different levels in the hierarchy of retail nucleations which is evident in empirical work in urban areas.[16]

[16]This may also be due to the dynamics of central place systems, since business types and retail nucleations change level through time. However, all adjustments to change are not immediate, but rather, there is a lagged reaction.

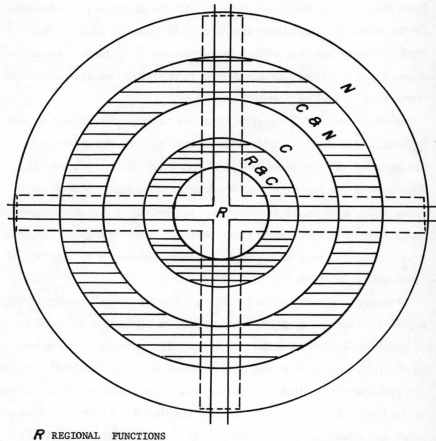

R REGIONAL FUNCTIONS
C COMMUNITY FUNCTIONS
N NEIGHBORHOOD FUNCTIONS

⌐ ⌐ ⌐ BOUNDARY OF NUCLEATION

FIGURE 23: HYPOTHETICAL INTERNAL STRUCTURE OF A REGIONAL NUCLEATION
BASED ON PRODUCT DIFFERENTIATION

CHAPTER V

THE RELATIONSHIP BETWEEN LAND VALUE AND LAND USE WITHIN RETAIL NUCLEATIONS

In this chapter, we turn to an analysis of the ground-floor arrangement of functions within the sample retail nucleations. The objective is to determine whether the hypothesized structure of business centers presented in the models is an adequate representation of the real world situation.

The Representation of Land Values

Evidence presented above suggests that the general level of land values at retail nucleations is in accord with their level in the hierarchy. Land values were also found to vary considerably within and between centers at different levels in the hierarchy. In general, high order centers are associated with high peak land values. Because of such variability, problems in the use of land values arises. When comparing values between centers at the same level in the hierarchy, there is no problem. However, serious distortions are introduced when cross-comparisons between centers at alternate levels are attempted.

Direct comparison of absolute land values is consequently

unsatisfactory. However, since values within nucleations reflect distance as a function of decreasing accessibility away from the peak intersection, they can be considered as relative to the peak lot value. Thus, each value can be represented as a percentage value of the peak lot. In this indexed form, values may be compared between centers at the same and at alternate levels in the hierarchy. Land values in this indexed form are used as the basis for the following discussion.[1]

The Representation of Threshold

Identification of the range in threshold values for each business type is not possible from the data available to the author. Moreover, it is even difficult to measure the value of the mean threshold for each individual business type. The methods used by Berry and Garrison to rank functions by absolute threshold size in Snohomish County, Washington, cannot be applied to similar studies in large urban areas because there is no such thing as a population: establishment ratio for retail nucleations.[2]

The use of a proxy variable to rank functions is, however, suggested from the relationships presented in Chapter I. Since the number of establishments of each business type decreases as threshold size increases, the lowest threshold type will at the same time be the most ubiquitous in the urban area. Therefore, a ranking of central functions

---

[1] For a more detailed explanation of this method, and an example of its use in analyzing internal structure, see B. J. Garner, "Land Values...," op. cit.

[2] B. J. L. Berry and W. L. Garrison, "Functional Bases...," op. cit.

by total number of establishments in the urban area should approximate
their ranking by threshold size.[3]

In this study, however, only the total number of establishments
occurring at each of the sixty-two retail nucleations is known. Moreover, the study is restricted to consideration of nucleated functions.
Many of these appear to be highly concentrated only at higher order
nucleations, although in actual number of establishments, they may be
equal to other types which are more widely dispersed between centers.
To overcome this, functions have been ranked by their frequency of
occurrence at retail nucleations. This ranking is shown in Table 26.

A note should be added about the ranking of functions in the table.
Firstly, functions are ranked according to their occurrence at all
sixty-two nucleations. Separate rankings are not identified for centers
in the Rest of the City and in the Workingmen's Areas, respectively.
Although this would perhaps be a desirable breakdown, preliminary
investigation showed that disaggregation of the data resulted in an ex-
cessive number of tied ranks. Because of this, it was difficult to
discriminate effectively between the order of functions.

Secondly, the high ranking of certain functions is not believed to
be an accurate representation of threshold size. This arises for either
of two reasons: (1) Upper-floor functions are underestimated; for
instance, photographic studios are predominantly in upper-floors at
high order centers and should perhaps be associated with a lower
threshold than is indicated by the frequency ranking; (2) Certain
functions, such as fish markets or fruit and vegetable stores, are
only marginal in retail nucleations and probably have a lower threshold
than indicated on account of their more frequent occurrence in
(a) ribbon developments, and (b) the smaller neighborhood centers
omitted from the study. Thus, the rank order of individual functions
is not believed to be identical to a ranking based upon exact

TABLE 26

CENTRAL FUNCTIONS RANKED BY FREQUENCY OF OCCURRENCE
AT RETAIL NUCLEATIONS IN THE CITY OF CHICAGO

(1)	(2)	Description	(1)	(2)	Description
4	5715	China and glasswear	31	5311	Department stores
5	5664	Children's shoes	33	5251	Hardware
6	5681	Furriers	33	5733	Music stores
6	5942	Book shops	33	7251	Shoe repairs
7	5699	Miscellaneous apparel	35	5422	Meat markets
7	7631	Watch repairs	35	5641	Children's wear
9	5423	Fish markets	35	5999	Miscellaneous retail
10	5431	Fruit and vegetables	35	6159	Personal loans
12	5633	Hosiery	36	7215	Laundromats
13	5634	Apparel accessories	37	783	Movie theaters
15	5719	Miscellaneous furniture	38	5732	Radio & television
16	5632	Lingerie	39	5411	Groceries
16	5996	Camera shops	41	60	Banks
16	7949	Sports promoter	42	5997	Gift & novelty
17	5713	Floor covering	43	'10	Supermarkets
17	5943	Stationers	44	5462	Bakeries
17	64	Insurance agents	44	8099	Optometrists
18	7221	Photographer	45	5441	Candy stores
19	5499	Delicatessen	48	5921	Liquor
20	5952	Sporting goods	49	5665	Family shoes
21	5631	Millinery	49	5712	Furniture
21	5651	Family clothes	49	5971	Jewelers
21	5993	Cigar stands	49	605	Currency exchange
22	5231	Paint and glass	50	7231	Beauty shops
22	5714	Drapery	51	5331	Variety
23	5392	Army and Navy stores	53	5621	Women's clothes
24	5722	Appliances	53	7211	Dry cleaners
27	5663	Women's shoes	54	5612	Men's clothes
28	5662	Men's shoes	58	5813	Bars
28	5992	Florists	61	5912	Drug stores
30	801	Medical services	62	5812	Eating places

Notes: (1) Number of centers at which function occurs.
(2) S.I.C. identification code.
'10 University of Chicago code numbering.

threshold sizes. However, evidence presented in Appendix D suggests
that the ranking by frequency of occurrence at centers is a viable
approximation of the ranking by mean threshold size.

The hypothesized internal structure of retail nucleations expressed
in the simple model is based upon the arrangement of functions by mean
threshold value. We must, therefore, relate these to the mean of the
range in land values for each individual function. The mean land value
is not, however, calculated for individual functions at each sample
center. Rather, centers sampled from each order or level in the
hierarchy have been grouped. The grand mean land value for each
function for the group of centers as a whole has been calculated.
Empirical verification of the hypotheses is, therefore, based upon the
analysis of the relationship between mean threshold size and mean land
value for each function by level of center. In this way, the generalizations presented relate to what is believed to be the structure of the
average center at each level in the hierarchy.

The Change in Mean Land Value for Functions
at Different Level Centers

It was hypothesized above that lower level functions will occur on
lower level values at higher order centers because they are displaced
outwards from the core area. The mean percent values for individual
functions at different level centers in the Rest of the City and in the
Workingmen's Area are shown in Table 27.

Superficially, it seems the data tends to support the validity of the
hypothesis. Low order functions are shown, in most cases, to be
displaced onto lower value land as order in the hierarchy increases.
However, this is not entirely true. For it is apparent that there is a
marked down-shift in the general level of percent values at the regional

TABLE 27

MEAN PERCENT LAND VALUES FOR FUNCTIONS BY LEVEL OF CENTER

S.I.C. Code	R	C	N	Major	Minor
5231 R	17.5	34.8	39.9	41.0	--
5251 N	23.5	45.4	36.3	34.4	11.3
5311 C	48.7	50.2	--	91.3	--
5331 C	41.3	60.5	60.1	46.6	48.0
5392 C	21.5	48.2	--	46.9	28.0
5411 N	22.8	58.6	46.7	31.8	43.7
10 N	19.0	38.7	45.3	--	39.0
5422 N	22.2	34.1	54.3	21.4	37.5
5423 N	14.2	--	--	11.8	30.0
5431 C	--	31.4	--	22.1	11.3
5441 C	49.1	54.2	54.2	63.3	25.6
5462 N	31.8	34.2	46.7	36.9	38.0
5499 C	28.8	58.5	--	--	22.0
5612 C	38.4	54.2	41.7	48.2	47.1
5621 C	41.3	50.4	37.5	50.4	28.0
5631 R	25.3	75.0	--	44.4	43.8
5632 R	32.5	--	46.7	49.9	--
5633 R	53.7	--	--	56.3	--
5634 R	56.2	37.5	--	56.3	--
5641 C	32.7	61.1	--	48.5	36.0
5651 C	44.1	44.5	--	26.9	44.3
5662 R	49.0	45.7	--	56.5	32.4
5663 R	43.7	72.4	--	51.5	43.8
5664 R	41.7	--	--	--	--
5665 C	39.3	54.5	--	49.5	52.3
5671 R	19.2	58.8	--	17.7	--
5699 R	32.0	32.9	--	--	--
5712 C	23.4	41.2	--	31.1	32.8
5713 R	22.4	51.3	--	28.0	--
5714 R	19.8	27.3	--	26.9	30.0
5715 R	15.1	19.6	--	--	--
5719 R	14.5	21.1	--	31.6	--
5722 R	31.8	49.7	--	38.9	--
5732 C	26.2	49.7	40.6	29.4	32.8
5733 C	19.6	35.4	--	44.1	43.8
5812 N	28.0	45.5	43.6	30.6	35.7
5813 N	19.6	45.3	43.4	17.9	47.2

TABLE 27 (cont'd.)

MEAN PERCENT LAND VALUES FOR FUNCTIONS BY LEVEL OF CENTER

S.I.C. Code	R	C	N	Major	Minor
			Level of Center		
5912 N	40.8	58.2	93.5	46.6	69.2
5921 C	22.1	51.0	45.1	20.6	32.2
5942 R	--	75.0	--	--	--
5943 C	18.3	41.7	--	26.0	--
5952 R	21.9	33.4	--	38.3	--
5971 C	35.3	47.0	46.7	42.8	25.6
5992 C	13.9	56.5	41.7	--	--
5993 R	--	100.0	--	59.5	100.0
5996 R	25.1	46.9	--	--	--
5997 C	24.5	40.2	30.7	36.3	28.0
5999 R	27.5	33.7	--	47.9	11.3
60 C	27.6	49.9	24.9	63.4	59.4
605 N	30.9	41.9	48.6	--	28.8
6159 C	25.8	44.6	55.8	23.4	37.5
64 R	24.1	23.2	--	--	--
65 N	20.1	39.8	38.9	--	28.8
7211 N	18.9	44.7	46.3	23.0	29.3
7215 N	17.7	41.1	42.7	--	23.2
7221 R	20.5	35.3	--	34.0	--
7231 N	19.3	44.5	38.6	17.5	--
7241 N	18.3	31.2	45.4	12.1	22.1
7251 N	14.7	41.8	26.1	--	35.0
7631 C	24.0	--	41.2	--	37.5
783 C	30.5	53.7	43.8	32.3	31.0
7949 R	28.2	--	--	--	--
801 N+	22.1	45.9	35.8	15.0	11.3
8099 N+	25.1	37.4	43.7	28.4	36.0
Vacant	21.7	43.2	71.4	32.1	37.3

Notes: R, C and N indicate regional, community and neighborhood level function and center, respectively.

N+ typical of the neighborhood level and all higher levels in the hierarchy.

centers. This arises on account of the disproportionately high peak values at the high order regional centers. Because of this, neighborhood and community functions always appear to be on lower value land when they occur at these centers. Similarly, when regional level functions occur at centers below that level, they always occur on higher value land. It is not, therefore, completely valid to discuss the values associated with neighborhood and community level functions when they occur at the regional centers. However, because there is no marked difference in value levels between the other centers, comparisons can be made about them without reservation.

Centers in the Rest of the City

In general, neighborhood functions are displaced onto lower value land when they occur at community centers. This is consistent with expectation. Bakeries illustrate this nicely. They are found on land valued at 46.7 percent of the peak at the neighborhood centers in which they are typical. They are displaced onto land valued at only 34.2 percent at the higher level community centers.

This is not, however, true for all neighborhood functions and it is perhaps more instructive to look at the deviant cases than those behaving as expected. Several neighborhood functions occur on higher value land when they occur at the community centers. They are namely: hardware, grocery, eating places, bars, real estate agents, beauty shops and shoe repairs. In the case of eating places and bars, deviation is probably the direct result of product differentiation at the higher level center. However, the same argument does not apply to the other business types. No immediate explanation is available for the higher values associated with hardware, grocery stores, beauty shops and shoe repairs. Real estate agents reflect, perhaps, the greater importance of the higher order centers in the provision of business services

and suggest that they are perhaps only marginal functions at the
neighborhood level.

Centers in the Workingmen's Area

There is less evidence of this regularity at the major and minor
centers. In part, this can be attributed to disturbances in land values
at these centers associated with decline of trade areas, and in part,
it is related to the lower level of demand serviced. For example, the
level of demand necessary to support a function at the community level
in the rest of the city may only be available at locations in the equivalent of regional (i.e., major) centers in this part of the city. Error in
classification may, therefore, cause disturbance of the regularity.

This would appear to be the case for women's clothes, jewelers,
banks, motion picture theaters and army and navy stores. These are
all considered to be typical of the community level in the Rest of the
City. But, they are all found on higher value land at major centers--
the equivalent of regional centers in the workingmen's area--than at
minor centers.

On the other hand, this is probably not the explanation for the
deviation of hardware stores in this part of the city. Although they are
classified as neighborhood functions, they also occur on higher value
land at major centers. Hardware stores were also noted to deviate at
centers in the Rest of the City where they occurred on higher value
land at the community level centers.

One explanation for this consistent deviation is suggested. Presumably, hardware stores are less important as independent suppliers
of hardware goods at higher order centers where they are in competition
with a variety of alternate suppliers. Variety stores, department stores
and even supermarkets offer a wide range of similar goods. If it can be
assumed that hardware stores become more specialized to counteract

this increased competition, it is conceivable that their rent-paying ability is increased, thereby enabling them to occupy higher value sites at higher order centers.

In general, lower order functions are displaced onto lower value land at higher order centers. However, it is difficult to say whether the hypothesis is supported at the regional level centers because of the down-shift in level of percent values. In spite of this, enough evidence is presented to lend general support to the hypothesis at the other centers.

Rank Order of Functions by Level of Center

It is perhaps more meaningful to generalize about relative changes in values for functions at higher order centers than to make statements about the absolute changes evident in Table 27. This is best done from the analysis of differences in the rank order of functions at each level of center. By doing this, comparisons can be made about location of lower order functions at higher order centers despite any changes in general level of percent values.

Thus, although percent values are generally lower at the regional centers, lower order functions should exhibit a similar ranking at this and lower level centers. Moreover, the analysis of changes in rank order enables verification of the hypothesis that functions typical of any given level are ordered among themselves according to threshold size.

In addition to merely ranking functions by percent value at each level in the hierarchy, functions have also been grouped on the basis of similarity of land values. Similarity in value between different functions is measured by the difference in land values between each function and all others in the array. The smaller the difference in value between any two functions, the greater their land value similarity, or, the greater their affinity for similar locations within retail nucleations. A matrix of value differences is formed, and functions are classified by the application of linkage analysis into groups comprising those activities showing the greatest similarity in land values.[4] In this way, not only can differences in the rank order of functions between alternate levels be investigated but at the same time it is possible to see any significant changes in the zonal arrangement of functions at the different level centers.

The rank order of functions is not expected to be identical for any two levels in the hierarchy. Sampling variability alone precludes this. However, significant differences in the ranking of functions can be detected by using Spearman rank correlation coefficients. Although minor changes may occur in the rank order of individual business types, these are not considered important unless they result in a significant difference in overall ranking when measured by rank correlation coefficients. Thus, a non-significant rank correlation is taken as an indication of dissimilarity between rankings.

Table 28 shows the ranking and zonal arrangement of neighborhood functions at the different levels of center. There does not appear to be a consistent pattern in arrangement from center to center. The changes in rank order of the neighborhood functions at the different centers can be summarized as follows:

(1) There is no significant difference between the overall ranking of functions at the neighborhood, regional, major and minor centers. However, the ranking of neighborhood level functions at the

[4]A more detailed discussion of this method and its application is found in B. J. Garner, "Notes on the Application of Nearest Neighbor Linkage Analysis," (mimeographed).

TABLE 28

CLUSTERING OF NEIGHBORHOOD LEVEL FUNCTIONS

Zone	Neighborhood	Community	Regional	Major	Minor	% Peak Value
I	Drugs				Drugs	60%
II	Meat Market	Grocery Drugs				50%
III	Currency X. Bakery Grocer Supermarket Barber Dry cleaner	Medical Eating place Bars Hardware		Drugs	Bars	45%
IV	Opticians Eating place Laundromats Bars	Dry cleaning Beauty shop Currency X. Shoe repairs Laundromats	Drugs		Grocer	40%
V	Real estate Beauty shop	Real estate Supermarket Opticians		Eating place	Supermarket Bakers Meat market	37%
VI	Hardware Medical	Bakery Meat market Barbers	Bakery Currency X.	Bakery Hardware Grocery	Optician Eating place Shoe repair	30%
VII	Shoe repair		Eating place Opticians Hardware Grocer Meat market Medical	Opticians Dry cleaners Meat market	Dry cleaner Real estate Currency X. Laundromat Barbers	20%
VIII			Bars Beauty shop Supermarket Dry cleaner Barbers Laundromats	Barbers Bars Beauty shop Medical		15%
IX			Shoe repairs Fish market	Fish market	Hardware Medical	

community centers is significantly different from that at all others.

(2) Although neighborhood functions as a group are concentrated in approximately the same value zones at neighborhood and community centers, they are displaced onto lower value zones at the regional level. In the Workingmen's centers, they are found on land intermediate in value to that at regional and community centers.

(3) The significant difference in rank order of neighborhood functions at the community level results from: (a) the higher ranking of hardware stores, groceries, eating places, bars, real estate offices and shoe repairs; and (b) the lower rank order of bakeries, barber shops, meat markets, currency exchanges and optometrists.

(4) Certain of these functions show consistent changes in rank order at other centers. Hardware stores rank much higher at regional and major centers, but rank much lower at minor centers. Real estate agents and shoe repairs also rank high at minor centers. Conversely, barber shops rank lower at regional centers, and meat markets much lower at major centers.

(5) Drug stores are outstanding in their consistently high rank order in all centers.

The rank order and zonal arrangement of community level functions are shown in Table 29. The more complex arrangement typical of higher order centers is immediately apparent. Notable differences in the arrangement of community level functions shown in the table can be summarized as follows:

(1) There is less regularity in zonal arrangement between different centers. At the regional level, functions are concentrated in the lower value zones, but are more dispersed at both the major and minor centers.

(2) The clustering of community functions into value zones is

TABLE 29

CLUSTERING OF COMMUNITY LEVEL FUNCTIONS

| Zone | Community | Level of Center | | | % Peak Value |
		Regional	Major	Minor	
I	Children's wear Variety		Dept. store Banks Candy		60%
II	Delicatessen Florist Family shoes Candy Men's clothes Movie theater			Bank Family shoes	52%
III	Liquor Dept. store Women's clothes		Women's clothes		50%
IV	Banks Radio - T.V.	Candy	Family shoes		49%
V	Army and Navy Jewelers	Dept. store	Children's wear Men's clothes Army and Navy	Variety Men's clothes	45%
VI	Loans Family clothes	Family clothes	Music Jewelers	Family clothes Music	42%
VII	Stationery Furniture Gifts	Women's clothes Variety	Variety		40%
VIII		Family shoes Men's clothes	Gifts	Loans Children's wear	36%
IX	Music Paint & Glass	Jewelers Children's wear Movie theater Delicatessen Banks	Movie theater Furniture Radio - T.V.	Furniture Radio - T.V. Liquor Movie theater Army and Navy Women's clothes Gifts	27%
X		Radio - T.V. Loans	Family clothes Stationery	Candy Jewelers	25%
XI		Gifts Furniture	Loans Fruit & veg.	Delicatessen	22%
XII		Liquor Army and Navy	Liquor		20%
XIII		Music Stationery Paint & Glass Florist			15%

less consistent between centers than is the case of the neighborhood level functions. In major centers, a completely different set of land value zones is evident.

(3) In spite of changes in zonal arrangement, community functions are ranked in essentially the same order at community, regional and major centers. The ranking at minor centers is, however, significantly different from that at all others.

(4) The difference in rank order at minor centers is due to changes in four functions: (a) family clothes and music stores which rank much higher, and (b) candy stores and delicatessens which rank much lower.

(5) Certain functions rank consistently higher or lower at centers other than the community level. These are: (a) banks, gift and novelty stores and members of the furniture group--radio and television stores, music stores and general furniture stores--which rank higher at all other centers, and (b) children's clothes stores, delicatessens, motion picture theaters and liquor stores which rank lower at all other centers.

(6) Certain other functions are characterized by a marked change in rank only at one other center. Thus, jewelers and family clothes stores rank higher at regional centers, and variety stores rank much lower at major centers. The extremely low rank order of florists at the regional level centers is presumed to be the result of sampling error.

Table 30 shows the ranking and zonal arrangement of regional level functions at the highest order centers. The basic difference in pattern is the change in zonal concentration at major centers where functions are clustered in higher value zones. However, in spite of this difference, there is a highly significant correlation between the two ranks. The distinction between an inner area of clothing functions

TABLE 30

CLUSTERING OF REGIONAL LEVEL FUNCTIONS

Zone	Regional	Major	% Peak Value
I	Apparel accessories	Cigar stand	
		Men's shoes	
		Hosiery	
		Apparel accessories	56%
	Hosiery		
	Men's shoes	Women's shoes	50%
II		Corsets and lingerie	
		Children's shoes	48%
	Women's shoes	Millinery	
III	Children's shoes	China and glass	40%
		Household appliances	
		Sports goods	35%
	Corsets and Lingerie		
IV	Misc. apparel	Photographers	
	Household appliances	Misc. furnishings	30%
		Floor covering	
	Sports promoters	Drapery	27%
V	Millinery		
	Cameras		
	Insurance		23%
	Floor covering		
VI	Sports goods		
	Photographers		
	Drapery		20%
VII	China and glass		
	Misc. furnishings		10%

and an outer area of furniture and other functions is clearly apparent at this level.

It is shown, therefore, that three basic differences exist in the rank order of each set of functions between alternate centers. These are: (1) the ordering of neighborhood functions at the community level is significantly different from the ranking at all other centers; (2) the ordering of community level functions at minor centers is significantly different from the ranking at all others; and (3) the ranking of neighborhood and community level functions is significantly different between major and minor centers.

Are Functions Ranked by Threshold?

Functions typical of each level in the hierarchy show, in general, similar rank order at the different centers. But, are they ranked by threshold size? In order to verify the hypothesis that high value functions are at the same time high threshold functions, rank correlations of the value and ubiquity scales were calculated for the set of neighborhood, community and regional level functions respectively at each center.

When all functions in any given array (e.g., all the neighborhood level functions at regional centers, or all the community level functions at major centers, etc.) are included in the calculation of the correlation coefficients, a significant correlation between value and threshold is found only at the neighborhood level. At these centers neighborhood functions are ranked according to expectation; high value neighborhood functions are high threshold functions.

At other centers, it becomes increasingly obvious that the measure of threshold used in this work is inadequate. Comparisons of the ranking by percent value and mean threshold size indicate that large differences in rank order occur for certain functions.

These functions are listed in Table 31. Two interesting generalizations

TABLE 31

FUNCTIONS WITH LARGE RANK DIFFERENCES

Community Centers	Regional Centers	Major Centers	Minor Centers
	Neighborhood Functions		
(b) Meat markets	(a) Hardware		
(a) Eating places	Eating places		Eating places
(a) Bars		Bars	
(a) Drug stores	Drug stores	Drug stores	Drug stores
(a) Currency exchange			
(a) Dry cleaners			
	(a) Laundromats		
(a) Beauty shops			
			(b) Medical services
	Community Functions		
(b) Paint and glass	Paint and glass		
(a) Variety stores	Variety stores		Variety stores
(a) Army and navy	Army & navy		Army & navy
			(b) Delicatessens
(a) Men's clothes	Men's clothes	Men's clothes	Men's clothes
	(a) Women's clothes	Women's clothes	
(b) Family clothes			
(a) Family shoes			
	Regional Functions		
	(a) Men's shoes	Men's shoes	
	(a) Women's shoes	Women's shoes	
	(b) China & Glassware		
	(b) Miscellaneous furnishings		

Note: (a) Functions with high mean value and low mean threshold.

(b) Functions with low mean value and high mean threshold.

can be made about them. Firstly, certain functions show large differences in rank order repeatedly at several centers. Secondly, some
functions are unique in that they deviate only at one center. With the
exception of paint and glass stores, functions deviating at more than
one center are characterized by a high mean value but a low threshold
index. They include eating places, bars, drug, variety and army and
navy stores, men's and women's clothes and shoe stores. The consistent deviation of these types at more than one center presumably
results from shortcomings in the measurement of mean threshold
rather than from sampling error in mean land value.

Measuring thresholds by frequency of occurrence at retail nucleations does not take into account shifts in scale of operation or product
differentiation of functions when they occur at higher level centers.
Thus, for example, many drug stores clearly change function at higher
levels in the hierarchy. They are usually larger scale operations providing a greater "bundle of goods" to the consumer, which in turn increases their latitude of product differentiation. However, this is not
revealed by the S.I.C. classification nor by the index of threshold used
in this work. Thus although drug stores are ubiquitous in the urban
area, there is presumably a marked upward shift in the range of
thresholds resulting in the ability to occupy higher value land. Similar
arguments can be extended to the other functions in this group.

In the case of paint and glass stores, the low frequency of occurrence would seem to be an overestimation of threshold size. This
activity is not a true central function since it occurs more frequently
in ribbons. Thus, the few establishments included by the method of
delimiting retail nucleations in this work is not an accurate index of
their degree of ubiquity in the urban area.

The remaining functions deviate at only one level. They include
functions similar to those above with high mean value and low threshold

index, such as laundromats, dry cleaners, currency exchanges and family stores, and conversely, functions with low mean value but a high threshold index, such as meat markets, hardware and family clothes stores. Deviation in the former case is presumed to be related to sampling error in mean land values. Many of these functions were noted to have changed rank considerably in the above analysis of rank orders. In the latter group, it would seem that threshold is overestimated.

Two high threshold furniture functions should be included in this list. China and glassware and miscellaneous furniture stores rank on low value land at the regional center although they are associated with a high threshold index. In this case, the difference in rank order is probably not related to error in sampling. Rather, it suggests the subtle difference between inter-and intra-center location. These functions need the centrality offered by high order centers--although this may be an intuitive conception. However, because of their large space needs and association with comparative shopping habits, they are unable to compete successfully for high value inner locations. Consequently, they are situated toward the periphery of high order centers where they are interspersed with lower order functions.

It is interesting to note that if, on the grounds of measurement error, these deviant cases are removed from the arrays, significant correlations are obtained. These are listed in Table 32. However, it is to be noted that even after removing deviant community level functions from the ranking at regional and minor centers, the two variables are still not significantly correlated.

TABLE 32

SIGNIFICANT RANK CORRELATIONS BETWEEN LAND VALUE
AND THRESHOLD SIZE

	Level of Center				
	N.	C.	R.	Major	Minor
Neighborhood functions	.45	.81	.60	.55	.63
Community functions	–	.52	x	.52	x
Regional functions	–	–	.71	.50	–

Notes: All correlations are significant at the five percent level.
   x represents the lack of significant correlation.
   – indicates that functions are not considered at that level.

Summary

   The rank order of functions at the different centers can be summarized as follows:

   (1) Apart from only one or two exceptions, functions typical of any given level in the hierarchy (i.e. neighborhood level functions, etc.), appear to be arranged in similar rank order when they occur at higher order centers. Furthermore, lower order functions are generally found on lower value land at higher order centers.

   (2) Certain functions are associated with minor changes in rank order at different centers. Since these changes do not destroy the overall ranking, they are presumed to be due to sampling error.

   (3) When allowance is made for shortcomings in the threshold index used in this work and sampling variation in land values, evidence suggests that functions trend toward a ranking by mean threshold size. Thus, in most cases, those functions which

have a high mean threshold also tend to be associated with a high mean land value.

(4) Shortcomings in the threshold estimation and in sampling error as reflected in the mean value, combine in such a way as to destroy the hypothesized relationship in the case of community level functions at regional and minor centers.

The Internal Structure of Nucleations

So far we have been dealing with the ranking of functions separately at different level centers. We now combine the rankings in order to test whether the pattern of internal arrangement hypothesized in the simple model is a valid representation of the real world nucleation. Generalizations about the internal structure of retail nucleations are made at two levels of data aggregation: firstly, the aggregate structure by S. I. C. major groups, and secondly, internal structure based on individual functions.

Neighborhood Centers. The average structure of neighborhood centers based on S. I. C. major groups is shown in Table 33. The variety group and personal loan offices rank first and second on land valued at 60.0 and 56.0 percent of the peak, respectively. These groups are not, however, typical of the neighborhood level, but are included to show that when higher order functions occur at lower order centers, they sometimes occupy higher value land than functions typical of that level. The high ranking of the groups comprising essentially neighborhood level functions--the food, miscellaneous and eating and drinking groups--is consistent with expectation. Personal services and hardware stores and medical services tend to be characteristic of the lower value peripheral part of neighborhood nucleations.

TABLE 33

THE INTERNAL STRUCTURE OF NEIGHBORHOOD CENTERS
BY S.I.C. GROUPS

S.I.C. Group	Description	Percent Value
53	Variety	60.1
6159	Loans	55.8
59	Miscellaneous	51.5
54	Food	49.4
605	Currency exchange	48.6
783	Motion picture theaters	43.8
58	Eating and drinking	43.5
56	Apparel	40.8
57	Furniture	40.6
72	Personal service	39.8
80	Medical services	39.8
65	Real estate agents	38.9
52	Hardware	38.1

The arrangement of individual functions within the neighborhood level centers is shown in Table 34. Drug stores are located on the highest value land at 93.5 percent of the peak value. This is expected since they are peak lot uses at this level. The predominant convenience nature of the neighborhood center is reflected in the location of food functions on sites above 45.0 percent of the peak. Hardware stores, personal services, with the exception of dry cleaners and barbers, medical services and real estate agents are found at the periphery on low value land.

The predictions of the model are verified at the neighborhood level where neighborhood functions occupy the core area of the nucleation. [5]

[5] In this and all other discussion of internal structure, high order functions are omitted from discussion when they occur at lower order centers. Thus here mention is made only of the neighborhood functions. Analysis indicates that when higher order functions appear at lower order centers, there is no significant correlation between their threshold size and land value location.

The ranking of functions by land value is significantly correlated with the ranking by threshold size ($R_s = .45$). The rather low coefficient is accounted for by the anomalous occurrence of meat markets on higher value land than is expected from threshold size, and to the low threshold index associated with eating places and bars.

TABLE 34

THE INTERNAL STRUCTURE OF NEIGHBORHOOD CENTERS

S.I.C. Code	Description	Percent Value	
5912	Drug stores	93.5	90.0%
5422	Meat markets	54.3	50.0%
605	Currency exchange	48.6	
5462	Bakeries	46.7	
5411	Grocers	46.6	
7211	Dry cleaners	46.3	
7241	Barbers	45.4	
10	Supermarkets	45.3	
8099	Optometrists	43.7	
5812	Eating places	43.6	
5813	Bars	43.4	
7215	Laundromats	42.7	40.0%
65	Real estate agents	38.9	
7231	Beauty shops	38.6	
5251	Hardware	36.3	
801	Medical services	35.8	30.0%
7251	Shoe repairs	26.1	

Community Centers. The structure of community level centers by S.I.C. major groups is shown in Table 35. Motion picture theaters and the apparel and variety groups are found on the highest value land. The food group is notably displaced onto lower value land at this level, where it is found in association with the personal service and hardware groups on land valued at approximately 40.0 percent of the peak. Banks and medical services are found between 45.0 percent and 50.0 percent of the peak, while the furniture group is located at the periphery on land at 36.9 percent of the peak value.

TABLE 35

THE INTERNAL STRUCTURE OF COMMUNITY CENTERS
BY S.I.C. GROUPS

S.I.C. Group	Description	Percent Value
783	Motion picture theaters	53.7
56	Apparel	53.2
53	Variety	53.0
59	Miscellaneous	51.1
60	Banks	49.9
801	Medical services	46.0
58	Eating and drinking	45.4
6159	Loans	44.7
54	Food	44.3
605	Currency exchange	41.9
72	Personal services	40.9
52	Hardware	40.1
65	Real estate	39.8
8099	Optometrists	37.4
57	Furniture	36.9

The arrangement of individual functions at community centers is shown in Table 36. According to the hypothesis, community level functions should occupy the high value inner core area, and should be surrounded by lower value land by the neighborhood level functions. The empirical evidence is quite convincing. With the exception of drug stores and groceries, which are interspersed among the higher value community level functions, neighborhood functions are notably concentrated toward the periphery of the nucleation on the lower value land. It is not surprising to find drug stores on high value land at this level, but there is no immediate explanation, apart from sampling error, for the high value location of grocery stores at this level.

TABLE 36

THE INTERNAL STRUCTURE OF COMMUNITY CENTERS

S.I.C.	Code	Description	Percent Value	
C	5641	Children's clothes	61.1	
C	5331	Variety stores	60.5	
				60.0%
N	5411	Grocers	58.6	
C	5499	Delicatessen	58.5	
C	5992	Florists	56.5	
C	5665	Family shoes	54.5	
C	5441	Candy	54.2	
N	5912	Drug stores	54.2	
C	5612	Men's clothes	54.2	
C	783	Motion picture theaters	53.7	
C	5921	Liquor stores	51.0	
C	5311	Department stores	50.0	
C	5621	Women's clothes	50.0	
				50.0%
C	60	Banks	49.9	
C	5732	Radio & Television	49.7	
C	5392	Army and navy stores	48.2	
C	5871	Jewelers	47.0	
N	801	Medical services	46.0	
N	5812	Eating places	45.5	
N	5251	Hardware	45.4	
N	5813	Bars	45.3	
N	7211	Dry cleaners	44.7	
C	6159	Loan offices	44.5	
N	7231	Beauty shops	44.5	
C	5651	Family clothes	44.5	
N	605	Currency exchanges	41.9	
N	7251	Shoe repairs	41.8	
C	5943	Stationery stores	41.7	
C	5712	Furniture	41.2	
N	7215	Laundromats	41.1	
C	5997	Gift and novelty stores	40.1	
				40.0%
N	65	Real estate agents	39.8	
N	10	Supermarkets	38.9	
N	8099	Optometrists	37.4	
C	5733	Music stores	35.4	
C	5231	Paints and glass	34.8	
N	5462	Bakeries	34.2	
N	5422	Meat markets	34.1	
N	7241	Barber shops	31.2	
				30.0%

Note: N and C represent neighborhood and community level functions respectively.

Conversely, community level functions are not all clustered in the core area; certain of them are located amongst the neighborhood functions on low value peripheral sites. In order of decreasing value, these are loan offices, family clothing stores, stationers, furniture, gift and novelty, and men's shoe stores. Loan offices are found more frequently on upper floors in the core area suggesting that they are perhaps unable to afford the higher value ground-floor core sites. Comparable rents are found only at some spots removed from the peak at the ground-floor level. There is no logical explanation for the occurrence of family clothing and stationery stores on low value land.

However, it is understandable why furniture stores should be found on low value locations. Because of their heavy reliance upon comparative purchasing, sales of furniture are not directly related to concentrations of buyers at the more central locations. This, together with their need for larger sites, forces furniture stores to locate at low rent peripheral sites.

Although the empirical evidence generally supports the predicted pattern of internal structure, it is not verified statistically. The lack of a significant correlation between values and thresholds can, however, be attributed to the disproportionately large difference in rank of a very small number of the thirty-six functions included in the initial correlation. If these are omitted from the calculation, a significant rank correlation of .34 is obtained.

Ten functions account for this difference. Five of these are functions for which it is believed thresholds are underestimated--namely, eating places, bars, drug stores, variety, men's and women's clothing stores. The other five would seem to be related to error from overlap in land values and include meat markets, candy stores, stationers, florists, and paint and glass stores.

These functions apart, the structure of community level centers is in general accordance with the hypothesis that the community functions are located in the high value core area, and are surrounded at the periphery by lower order neighborhood functions.

Regional Centers. The structure of the regional level centers based on S. I. C. major groups is shown in Table 37. Apart from the lower level of values, the pattern is not radically different from the aggregate structure of the community centers.[6]

TABLE 37

THE INTERNAL STRUCTURE OF REGIONAL CENTERS
BY S. I. C. GROUPS

S. I. C. Group	Description	Percent Value
56	Apparel	39. 2
53(1)	Variety	37. 1
605	Currency exchange	30. 9
783	Motion picture theaters	30. 5
54	Food	28. 3
60	Banks	27. 6
6159	Loans	25. 8
8099	Optometrists	25. 1
64	Insurance	24. 1
58	Eating and drinking	23. 8
801	Medical services	22. 1
57	Furniture	21. 6
59	Miscellaneous	21. 5
52	Hardware	20. 5
65	Real estate agents	20. 1
72	Personal services	18. 2

Notes: (1) This includes 5392 (army and navy stores). When this is omitted, the 53 group ranks first with a value of 44. 9 percent.

[6] This is an interesting finding since B. J. L. Berry states, "Functions performed (at regional centers) differ from community centers not so much in types included, as in their number and variety." See B. J. L. Berry and R. M. Lillibridge, "Guides for the Provision...," op. cit., p. 12.

The clothing and variety groups, and motion picture theaters again rank on the highest value land. However, they are joined at this level by currency exchanges, which ranked somewhat lower at the community level. The most noticeable difference in arrangement at this level is the location on lower value sites of the personal service and miscellaneous groups. Medical services are also found on low value ground-floor sites at regional centers. At this level, they are more commonly found at centrally located upper floors, where they constitute older, upper-floor medical complexes.

Table 38 shows the relative location of individual functions in regional centers. The arrangement is much more complex than the geometry hypothesized in the simple model. Regional, community and neighborhood functions are not concentrated in discrete zones of decreasing value land. Rather, evidence suggests that functions typical of each level are interspersed with each other to form zones of overlapping land use according to the more complex model.

Neighborhood functions are, generally speaking, clustered toward the periphery, although perhaps not as noticeably as at the community level center. Notable exceptions are drug stores, bakeries, eating places and optometrists. These are interspersed with high order functions in the core area. Community level functions are highly scattered throughout the center. Some of them are interspersed with the regional functions on high value land. Notable among these are candy stores, department and variety stores and jewelers.

Only the regional level clothing functions are concentrated in the core area. Some are found at the periphery in association with neighborhood level functions. This is especially true of photographic studios, sports goods stores, and members of the furniture group, including floor covering, drapery stores, china and glassware and miscellaneous furniture stores. Field investigation suggests that

TABLE 38

THE INTERNAL STRUCTURE OF REGIONAL CENTERS

S. I. C.	Code	Description	Percent Value	
R	5634	Apparel accessory	56.2	
R	5633	Hosiery stores	53.7	50.0%
C	5441	Candy	49.1	
R	5662	Men's shoes	49.0	
C	5311	Department stores	48.7	
C	5651	Family clothes	44.1	
R	5663	Women's shoes	43.7	
R	5664	Children's shoes	41.7	
C	5621	Women's clothes	41.3	
C	5331	Variety stores	41.3	
N	5912	Drug stores	40.8	40.0%
C	5665	Family shoes	39.3	
C	5612	Men's clothes	38.4	
C	5971	Jewelers	35.3	
R	5641	Children's clothes	32.7	
R	5632	Corset and lingerie	32.5	
R	5699	Miscellaneous clothing	32.0	
R	5722	Household appliances	31.8	
N	5462	Bakeries	31.8	
N	605	Currency exchanges	30.9	
C	783	Motion picture theaters	30.5	30.0%
C	5499	Delicatessen	28.8	
R	7949	Sports promoters	28.2	
N	5812	Eating places	28.0	
C	60	Banks	27.6	
C	5732	Radio & Television	26.2	
C	6159	Loan offices	25.8	
R	5631	Millinery stores	25.3	
N	8099	Optometrists	25.1	
R	5996	Camera stores	25.1	
C	5997	Gift and novelty	24.5	
R	64	Insurance	24.1	
C	7631	Watch repairs	24.0	
N	5251	Hardware	23.5	
C	5712	Furniture	23.4	
N	5411	Grocers	22.8	
R	5713	China and glassware	22.4	
N	5422	Meat markets	22.2	
C	5921	Liquor stores	22.1	
N	801	Medical services	22.1	
R	5952	Sporting goods stores	21.9	
C	5392	Army and navy stores	21.5	
R	7221	Photographers	20.5	
N	65	Real estate agents	20.1	20.0%

TABLE 38 - Continued

S.I.C. Code		Description	Percent Value
R	5714	Drapery stores	19.8
C	5733	Music stores	19.6
N	5813	Bars	19.6
N	7231	Beauty shops	19.3
N	10	Supermarkets	19.0
N	7211	Dry cleaners	18.9
N	7241	Barbers	18.3
C	5943	Stationery stores	18.3
N	7215	Laundromats	17.7
C	5231	Paint and glass stores	17.7
R	5715	Floor covering	15.1
N	7251	Shoe repairs	14.7
R	5719	Miscellaneous furnishing	14.5
N	5423	Fish and sea foods	14.2
C	5992	Florists	13.9

Note: R, C and N indicate regional, community and neighborhood level functions respectively.

photographic studios, like medical services and personal loan offices, are more commonly found on upper floors in the core area. In order to locate on comparable value sites at the ground-floor level, they must move outwards toward the periphery. If it can be assumed that comparative shopping habits are associated with the purchase of sports goods as well as furniture items, the peripheral location of these functions can also be explained in terms of buying habits.

The most notable features in the arrangement of functions within regional centers can be summarized as follows:

(1) There is a marked concentration of clothing functions in the high value core area. This not only comprises the more specialized regional level but also the more general community level types.

(2) Peripheral sites are occupied by personal services and food functions together with certain members of the regional level furniture group.

(3) Between these extremes, the body of the center is characterized by a complex mix of community and regional level functions in which the miscellaneous group and financial services are significant.

The more complex arrangement of functions within the center is reflected by the lack of a significant rank correlation between value and threshold. When all functions are included, the coefficient is only .19. However, as was the case at the community level, this low coefficient is due, in large part, to large differences in rank order for one or two individual types. If these are omitted from the calculation, a significant correlation of .63 is obtained.

The observations exerting a distorting effect on the hypothesized relationship fall into two groups. Firstly, candy stores, women's clothes, variety, drug stores and men's clothes stores deviate because of underestimated threshold size. Presumably, scale shifts resulting in steep rent-bid curves enable them to compete for high value core

locations in spite of their high degree of ubiquity in the urban area.
Secondly, there is a group of functions for which it seems that the
mean land value is under or overestimated. This includes watch repairs, paint stores, china and glass stores, miscellaneous home
furnishings, florists and fish markets.

Deviation in the case of watch repairers and miscellaneous furnishings may, however, be related to shortcomings in the S. I. C.
classification rather than to error in the mean value. Most jewelers
offer watch repair services to their customers. However, classification by dominant line of business identifies these as jewelers and not
as watch repairers. Establishments whose sole function is the repair
of watches occur infrequently in the urban area. Hence, occurring at
few nucleations, they are recorded as high threshold functions using
the method adopted in this work. Similarly, miscellaneous furniture
stores comprise establishments which do not have any dominant line
of business. Since these are also few in number, they too appear as
high threshold functions because of their low frequency of occurrence
at centers.

Apart from the distorting effects that these functions have on the
ranking by value and threshold, the pattern of arrangement of functions
at the regional level is in general accord with the hypothesized
arrangement. However, considerable overlap between different level
functions is apparent. This is presumably a reflection of product
differentiation and its effect upon the mean land value for individual
functions.

Workingmen's Centers. The internal structure of major and
minor centers by S. I. C. major groups is shown in Tables 39 and 40,
respectively. The patterns are basically similar. The variety group
and banks are found on the highest value land, and personal services
and medical services are found on the lowest value land at both centers.

TABLE 39

THE INTERNAL STRUCTURE OF MINOR CENTERS BY S.I.C. GROUPS

S.I.C. Group	Description	Percent Value
60	Banks	59.4
53 (1)	Variety	48.0
59	Miscellaneous	41.6
58	Eating and drinking	41.4
56	Apparel	40.9
6159	Loans	37.5
8099	Optometrists	36.0
57	Furniture	34.8
783	Motion picture theaters	31.0
54	Food	30.9
72	Personal services	29.4
65	Real estate agents	28.8
605	Currency exchange	28.8
52	Hardware	11.3
801	Medical services	11.3

Note: (1) 5932 (Army and navy stores) excluded.

TABLE 40

THE INTERNAL STRUCTURE OF MAJOR CENTERS BY S.I.C. GROUPS

S.I.C. Group	Description	Percent Value
60	Banks	63.4
53 (1)	Variety	59.7
56	Apparel	46.4
59	Miscellaneous	38.0
52	Hardware	37.7
57	Furniture	33.0
783	Motion picture theaters	32.3
54	Food	31.2
8099	Optometrists	28.4
58	Eating and drinking	27.8
6159	Loans	23.4
72	Personal services	21.7
801	Medical services	15.0

Note: (1) 5932 (Army and navy stores) excluded.

The food group is also typical of low value locations.

Two notable differences exist. The eating and drinking group ranks high in value at minor centers. As was pointed out above, there is an exceptional concentration of eating places and bars at minor centers, and it is significant that they appear on high value land. Conversely, hardware stores rank much higher in value at major centers.

The arrangement of individual functions within minor centers is shown in Table 41. Although some neighborhood functions cluster on low value land, they are generally more dispersed among the community level functions on higher value land. There is little evidence of community level functions occupying the high value core of the nucleation. Although the few regional level functions appearing at minor centers do not cluster as a group in the innermost part of the nucleation, they nevertheless tend to occupy higher value sites.

Cigar stores and drug stores occupy the highest value sites. Bars are located on high value inner locations in the same way as at the neighborhood centers. The food group also ranks high at this center, especially groceries, supermarkets, bakeries and meat markets. These are only found at locations of comparable value at neighborhood centers in the Rest of the City.

High value community level functions include banks and representatives of the clothing functions--family shoes, men's and family clothing stores. Furniture stores appear on relatively high value land at these centers. This is in direct contrast to their location at the community level to which the minor center is assumed to be functionally equivalent.

The arrangement of individual functions at major centers is shown in Table 42. A more complex pattern is immediately evident. Its most significant feature is the dispersed location of the regional level functions. Apart from the clustering of clothing functions on the innermost

TABLE 41

THE INTERNAL STRUCTURE OF MINOR CENTERS

S.I.C.	Code	Description	Percent Value	
R	5993	Cigar stands	100.0	
N	5912	Drug stores	69.2	60.0%
C	60	Banks	59.4	
C	5665	Family shoes	52.3	50.0%
C	5331	Variety stores	48.0	
N	5813	Bars	47.2	
C	5612	Men's clothes	47.1	
C	5651	Family clothes	44.3	
R	5663	Women's shoes	43.8	
R	5631	Millinery	43.8	
N	5411	Grocers	43.7	
C	5733	Music stores	43.7	40.0%
N	10	Supermarkets	39.0	
N	5462	Bakeries	38.0	
N	5422	Meat markets	37.5	
C	7631	Watch repairs	37.5	
C	6159	Loans	37.5	
N	8099	Optometrists	36.0	
C	5641	Children's clothes	36.0	
N	5812	Eating places	35.7	
N	7251	Shoe repairs	35.0	
C	5712	Furniture	32.8	
C	5732	Radio & Television	32.8	
R	5662	Men's shoes	32.4	
C	5921	Liquor stores	32.2	
-	5934	Secondhand furniture	31.3	
C	783	Motion picture theaters	31.0	
N	5423	Fish markets	30.0	
R	5714	Drapery stores	30.0	30.0%
N	7211	Dry cleaners	29.3	
-	5939	Secondhand stores	29.2	
N	65	Real estate agents	28.8	
N	605	Currency exchange	28.8	
C	5392	Army and navy stores	28.0	
C	5621	Women's clothes	28.0	
C	5997	Gift shops	28.0	
C	5441	Candy	25.6	
C	5971	Jewelers	25.6	
N	7215	Laundromats	23.2	
N	7241	Barbers	22.1	
C	5499	Delicatessen	22.0	20.0%
N	5251	Hardware	11.3	
N	801	Medical services	11.3	
C	5431	Fruit and vegetable stores	11.3	

Note: R, C and N indicate regional, community and neighborhood level functions
respectively.

TABLE 42

THE INTERNAL STRUCTURE OF MAJOR CENTERS

S.I.C. Code			Percent Value	
C	5311	Department stores	<u>91.3</u>	90.0%
C	60	Banks	63.7	
C	5441	Candy	<u>63.3</u>	60.0%
R	5993	Cigar stands	59.5	
R	5662	Men's shoes	56.5	
R	5633	Hosiery	56.3	
R	5634	Apparel accessory	56.3	
R	5663	Women's shoes	51.5	
C	5621	Women's clothes	50.4	
R	5632	Corset and lingerie	<u>50.0</u>	50.0%
C	5665	Family shoes	49.5	
C	5641	Children's clothes	48.5	
C	5612	Men's clothes	48.2	
C	5392	Army and navy stores	46.9	
C	5331	Variety stores	46.6	
N	5912	Drug stores	46.4	
R	5631	Millinery	44.4	
C	5733	Music stores	44.1	
C	5971	Jewelers	42.8	
R	5231	Paint and glass stores	<u>41.0</u>	40.0%
N	5462	Bakeries	36.9	
R	5722	Appliances	39.8	
R	5952	Sports goods stores	38.3	
C	5997	Gift and novelty	36.3	
N	5251	Hardware	34.4	
R	7221	Photographers	34.0	
C	783	Motion picture theaters	32.3	
N	5411	Grocers	31.8	
R	5719	Miscellaneous furniture	31.6	
C	5712	Furniture	31.1	
N	5812	Eating places	<u>30.6</u>	30.0%
C	5732	Radio & television	29.4	
N	8099	Optometrists	28.4	
R	5713	Floor covering stores	28.0	
R	5714	Drapery stores	27.0	
C	5651	Family clothes	27.0	
C	5943	Stationers	26.0	
C	6159	Loan offices	23.4	
N	7211	Dry cleaners	23.0	
N	5431	Fruit and vegetables	22.1	
N	5422	Meat markets	21.4	
C	5921	Liquor stores	<u>20.6</u>	20.0%
N	5813	Bars	17.9	
N	7231	Beauty shops	17.5	
N	801	Medical services	15.0	
N	7241	Barbers	12.1	
N	5423	Fish markets	11.8	

Note: R, C and N indicate regional, community and neighborhood level
functions respectively.

high value sites, the rest are scattered on lower value land toward the periphery, where they are interspersed with neighborhood and community functions.

The highest value land is occupied by department stores, banks, candy stores and cigar stands. Following these there is a notable concentration of clothing functions, comprising the more specialized regional level types--men's shoes, hosiery, apparel accessory, women's shoes, infants' wear, and the more general community level men's and women's clothes stores. Family clothes stores are, however, not included in this group, but are found toward the periphery on lower value land. Drug and variety stores are also displaced onto relatively lower value land at these centers. In general, furniture functions are found on low value sites, although this is not true of music stores and household appliances. These are both found on higher value land in the middle parts of the nucleation. At the periphery, low value sites are occupied by representatives of the personal services and food group of functions.

The empirical evidence does not support the hypothesized pattern. High order functions neither cluster in the inner high value sites, nor are they surrounded by lower order functions on lower value land. The pattern is considerably more complex; functions typical of each level are markedly dispersed throughout centers.

A suggested reason for the considerable overlap in arrangement is the poverty of the S. I. C. classification. Functions have probably been mis-classified by level at Workingmen's centers owing to the reduced level of demand serviced. For instance, although a function may be classified as typical of a community center in the Rest of the City, it may not be typical of the equivalent level center in the Workingmen's area. Hence, taxonomic error would easily destroy regularity in functional arrangement.

The lack of visual regularity in the tables is also reflected in a lack of a significant statistical correlation between land values and thresholds at major and minor centers. However, if certain deviating functions are omitted from the calculation at minor centers, a significant coefficient of .46 is obtained. Functions for which there is a large difference in rank order are hardware, variety and fruit stores, delicatessens, men's clothes, family shoes and drug stores, bars, banks and medical services. Similarly, a significant rank correlation of .51 is found at major centers if deviating functions are removed. These include department stores, fish markets, candy, men's, women's and family clothes stores, floor covering and miscellaneous furniture stores, gift shops and banks.

Five of these functions were listed above as having an under-estimated threshold value. The rest appear to deviate more because of irregularities of mean value than of threshold. It is likely that these are the functions which have been misclassified since they assume a different level in the Workingmen's area on account of the lower level of demand serviced. For instance, banks have large differences in rank order at both major and minor centers because of their high value. Presumably, they become high rent-paying functions in place of the more specialized activities which are not present at these centers. Family clothes and family shoe stores are other types for which a similar argument seems to apply. However, more detailed analyses of the shift in level of functions associated with areal differences in socio-economic characteristics are needed before valid generalizations of this sort can be meaningfully proposed.

Therefore, there is less empirical evidence to support the hypothesized geometrical arrangement at these centers than at those in the Rest of the City. This is presumed to arise from shortcomings in classification. Consequently, there is no statistical verification of the hypotheses at major and minor centers.

Similarities in Internal Structure between Centers in the Rest of the City and Workingmen's Area

In spite of shortcomings in the data, some statements can be made about the similarities in internal structure of major and minor centers with those in the Rest of the City. It was shown that minor centers tend to be most like community centers, and major centers most like regional centers in functional structure. The same analogy exists with respect to their internal structure, although, perhaps, a little less clearly. Nevertheless, in both minor and community level centers, neighborhood functions tend to cluster on low value land at the periphery. This is, however, more apparent at community than at minor centers. In the latter, neighborhood functions are found in some cases on inner, high value sites.

The major difference between the two patterns is in the location of the food group of functions which are more clustered on higher value land at minor than at the community centers. This presumably reflects the more important role of convenience functions at minor centers. Apart from bars, which enjoy a rather anomolous position on high value land at minor centers, similar functions occupy high value sites in both centers. In other respects the two types of center show a high degree of similarity in internal structure.

There is more similarity between the major centers and the regional centers. In both, the high value core sites are occupied by the general and more specialized clothing functions, department stores, candy, variety and drug stores. The same kinds of functions are also typical of low value locations at both centers and include a variety of personal services and food functions. One notable difference is in the location of furniture stores. These are peripheral uses at regional centers, but are notably concentrated at sites intermediate to the high and low values at major centers.

Summary

At each of the five centers studied, the empirical evidence presented tends to support the hypothesized internal structure of retail nucleations. Allowing for shortcomings in the classification of functions, the effect of sampling error on land values, and the under- and over-estimation of thresholds by the proxy variable used in this study, mean land values and mean threshold size tend to be significantly correlated at each center. It must be concluded, therefore, that there is some general underlying order to the arrangement of retail activities within retail nucleations. This order is founded on the premise that high mean threshold functions are at the same time high rent-paying functions, and therefore are found in association with high mean land values. Thus, generally speaking, high order functions occupy the innermost, high value part of the nucleation at any level in the hierarchy, and are surrounded concentrically by the sets of functions typical of each preceding lower level. The occurrence of lower order functions on high value land is accounted for by increased rent-paying ability at higher order centers arising from scale shifts and product differentiation.

Range in Land Values of Functions

All establishments of a given type are not concentrated at the same location within retail nucleations. They are dispersed in varying degrees throughout them. The extent of dispersion varies directly with the degree of product differentiation between establishments. Because of this, each establishment has its own individual and unique threshold size, and a range of thresholds is created for each business type. Lower order functions are thereby enabled to compete with higher order functions for locations whenever their threshold ranges overlap. Thus, the apparently complex internal structure of retail nucleations can be rationalized.

Translated into land value terms, the range in thresholds is presumably reflected in the dispersion of land values about the mean values used in the above analysis. Although data is not available to determine the threshold range of each function, the range in land values for each function can be empirically determined. Since there is, in general, a direct relationship between mean thresholds and mean land values, the range in value can be substituted as a proxy variable for the threshold range. Using this information, the fundamentals of the pattern of functional dispersion, and the extent to which different functions overlap as postulated in the more complex model, can be appreciated.

Absolute Variability in Land Values

Figures 24, 25 and 26 show the absolute range in land values for functions at neighborhood, community and regional level centers respectively. In the figures, functions are arrayed horizontally from left to right in order of decreasing mean land value. The absolute range in value is represented by the vertical columns, the upper and lower limits of which are equal to the highest and lowest value associated with a function at any of the sample centers respectively. The top of the figure corresponds to the value 100 percent, ergo it is a diagrammatic representation of the peak lot. For our purposes, we assume that an establish ment is able to compete for any location along the value range. When a function occurs only once at the sample centers, and consequently has no range in values, it is plotted on the figure by its mean value only.

The extent of overlap between functions in the real world is more complex than was indicated in the conceptual discussion of threshold ranges above. Although it is difficult to generalize about the diagrams,

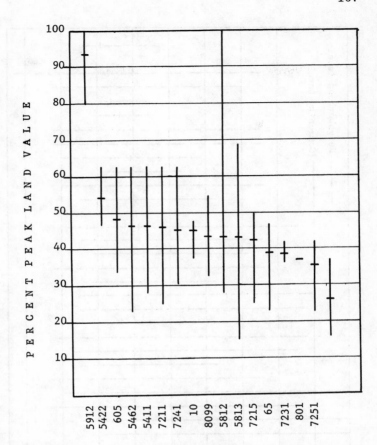

FIGURE 24: RANGE IN LAND VALUES OF NEIGHBORHOOD FUNCTIONS AT THE
NEIGHBORHOOD LEVEL

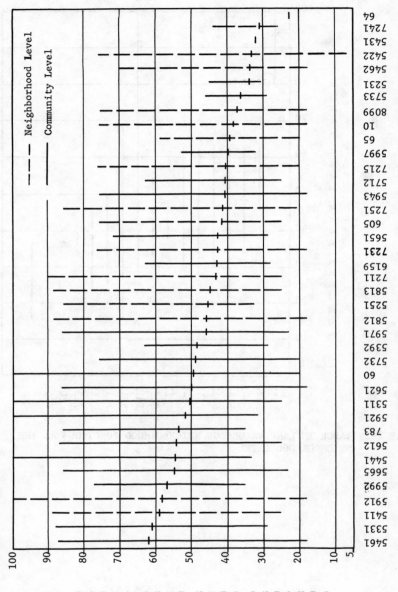

FIGURE 25: RANGE IN LAND VALUES OF FUNCTIONS AT COMMUNITY LEVEL NUCLEATIONS

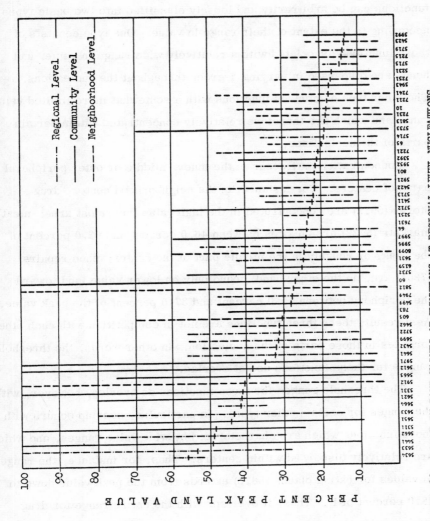

FIGURE 26: RANGE IN LAND VALUES OF FUNCTIONS AT REGIONAL LEVEL NUCLEATIONS

functions can be arbitrarily and loosely classified into two basic types according to the extent of their range in value. One type consists of those functions associated with a relatively wide range in value, and hence are dispersed in varying degrees throughout the nucleations. The other type comprises functions with a somewhat more limited value range and which are therefore relatively concentrated within certain parts of the nucleations.

Concentration may occur in the inner, middle or outer peripheral parts of centers. For instance, in the neighborhood center, drug stores (5912) are concentrated in the high value innermost area; meat markets (5422) are on sites between 46.0 percent and 62.0 percent of the peak, or roughly in the middle part of the center; shoe repairs (7251) are, on the other hand, found only on lower value land toward the periphery between 15.0 percent and 37.0 percent of the peak value. As a result, these three functions are not in competition with each other for sites in those parts of the nucleation. In other words, the threshold ranges for these functions do not overlap.

The threshold ranges for these functions do overlap, however, with the ranges for certain other types. In particular, overlap occurs with those functions which are characterized by wide value ranges, and which are relatively dispersed within centers. Thus, for instance, the range in values for eating places (5812) extends from the peak value down to 28.0 percent of it. Thus, it overlaps with the entire range for drug stores and meat markets, and with the uppermost part of the range for shoe repairs. Competition presumably exists between these functions for sites at different parts of the nucleation.

In general, there is a marked increase in the range of values for most functions as order in the hierarchy increases. This is to be expected since it has already been shown that functions occur most frequently at higher order centers on account of the larger portion of the urban markets serviced by them. Wide differences in tastes, needs and preferences of the individuals comprising this demand presumably allows scale shifts and a greater degree of product differentiation between establishments.

Thus at higher order centers, thresholds for any given function extend over a greater range. This is expressed geographically by the increased dispersion of lower order functions within high order centers. For instance, neighborhood functions by and large are more dispersed-- or extend over a wider range of values--when they occur at the community level. Drug stores, which were notably concentrated on high value land at neighborhood level centers, are found on land as low as 18.0 percent of the peak value at the higher order center. The resulting effect is an increase in the number of different functions competing for sites at any single part of the nucleation.

This is clearly illustrated by the increase in the type of functions competing for peak lot locations at the higher order centers. At the neighborhood level, only drug stores and eating places are in competition for peak lots. Five functions compete for these at the community centers. Drug stores are again represented, and are joined by candy, liquor and department stores, and banks. It appears that eating places are unable to meet the increased competition for these high value sites at this level, although their absence probably reflects sampling variability. Competition is even more acute at the regional level where nine functions occupy peak lots. Apart from liquor stores, which are not represented at this level, hosiery, variety, women's clothes and jewelry stores are added to those functions present at the community level. It is interesting to note that eating places reappear as peak lot occupants at this level although they were absent at the previous one.

Neighborhood Centers. Figure 24 shows that eating places and bars extend over the greatest range in values at this level center.

Their ranges do not, however, overlap at the highest and lowest extremities. Eating places are in competition with drug stores at locations valued at above 80.0 percent of the peak; whereas bars compete with shoe repairs on the lower value land below 23.0 percent of the peak. Most functions at this level are in competition for sites between 30.0 percent and 60.0 percent of the peak, although the range for individual functions does not always extend fully between these limits. For instance, supermarkets and beauty shops appear relatively concentrated between 37.0 percent and 49.0 percent, and 36.0 and 41.0 percent of the peak value respectively where they are in competition with other types.

Community Centers. The major difference at this level is the greater geographical dispersion of functions, as shown in Figure 25. Although the range in value varies considerably between individual types, only four functions are characterized by ranges which are small enough for them to be considered concentrated within the nucleation. These are gift shops (5997), music stores (7235), paint and glass stores (5231), and to a lesser extent, barber shops (7241). Other functions, generally speaking, extend between 25.0 percent and 85.0 percent of the peak value. Five functions occupy peak lot locations. At the periphery, meat markets (5422) stand in isolation on land below 18.0 percent of the peak. It is significant that the range in values increases for all the neighborhood level functions when they occur at the community centers.

Regional Centers. Figure 26 shows the distribution of functions at the highest order center. The down-shift in value is reflected in the extension of virtually all functions onto land valued below 20.0 percent of the peak value. There is consequently, less competition for high value sites.

Apart from the nine functions mentioned as peak-lot occupiers, only a handful of other activities extend onto land above 60.0 percent of the peak. These consist of representatives of the clothing group of functions, although not all types in this group are included. For instance, children's clothes (5641), apparel accessories (5631), children's shoes (5664) and millinery stores (5631), all have upper limits below the 60.0 percent level. Apparel accessories and children's shoes are the most concentrated of all the clothing functions. The former are concentrated between 60.0 percent and 52.0 percent of the peak; the latter between 48.0 percent and 35.0 percent. They are the only two clothing functions for which values ranges do not overlap, and which are therefore not in competition for site utility.

Other notably concentrated functions include, hardware stores (5251), located between 20.0 percent and 30.0 percent of the peak; and two regional level representatives of the furniture group, china and glassware stores (5715) and miscellaneous furnishings (5719), both of which are found below 20.0 percent of the peak at the periphery of the nucleation. In general, other functions at this level show varying degrees of geographical dispersion.

Workingmen's Centers. Figures 27 and 28 show the range in values for functions at the minor and major centers respectively. The data is much more incomplete at minor centers because many functions occur only once at sample centers. In spite of this, some generalizations can be made.

At minor centers there is a distinct difference in the extent of value ranges between the high and low mean value functions. A somewhat similar situation was noted at the neighborhood level. High value functions tend to be more dispersed; whereas lower value functions are usually more concentrated. Dispersed high value functions include drug stores (5912), bars (5813), banks (60), men's clothes (5612) and family clothes stores (5651). Family shoe stores are exceptions to

174

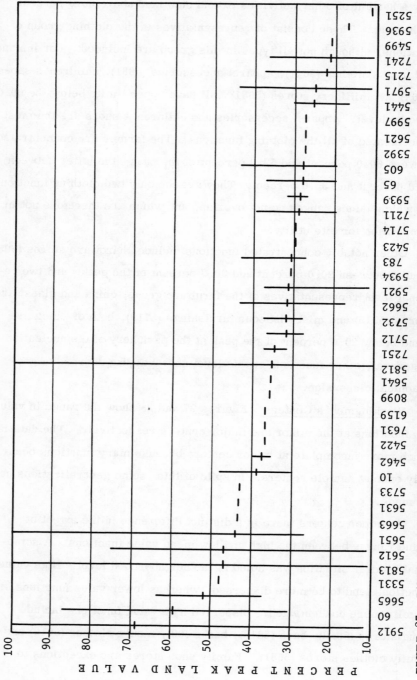

FIGURE 27: RANGE IN LAND VALUES OF FUNCTIONS AT MINOR CENTERS

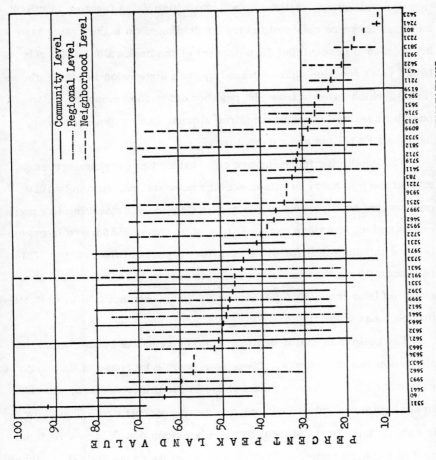

FIGURE 28: RANGE IN LAND VALUES OF FUNCTIONS AT MAJOR NUCLEATIONS

this generalization. Although they are a high value function in minor centers, they are relatively more concentrated on higher value land between 45.0 percent and 65.0 percent of the peak value. The only lower value function characterized by such dispersion is eating places (5812), which extends from the peak lot out to the periphery. Five peak lot uses are recognized: drug stores, family clothes stores, bars, eating places and candy stores.

The remaining functions are concentrated in varying degrees toward the periphery of minor centers between approximately 10.0 percent and 40.0 percent of the peak. Considerable overlap in ranges exists and all functions except family shoe stores (5665) are in competition with each other for sites at different parts of the center. This is especially marked in the lower value part of the nucleation. However, on land above 50.0 percent of the peak, competition is restricted to high mean value types.

The pattern at major centers in many respects is similar to that at the community centers. There is a notable increase in the range in values for all functions. Unlike those in the minor centers, the relatively high mean value functions are more concentrated. Thus, for instance, department stores (5311) only extend out as far as 70.0 percent of the peak value, and overlap between its range and others takes place notably between 70.0 percent and 80.0 percent of the peak. Other functions concentrated on higher value land include banks (60), women's shoe stores (5663), candy stores (5441), cigar stands (5993), and to a lesser extent, men's shoe stores (5662).

Most functions are fairly well dispersed between 70.0 percent and 20.0 percent of the peak value. Functions overlap considerably between these limits. Two functions stand out as being relatively more dispersed within this area. Women's clothes stores (5621) and drug stores (5912) both extend onto higher value land and occupy peak lots. Other peak-lot functions are department stores (5311), and candy stores (5441). It is interesting to note that the number of functions in competition for peak lots at the higher level center is the same as at minor centers. This is directly reverse to the situation at centers in the Rest of the City, where there was an increase in the number of peak lot uses as order in the hierarchy increased.

Functions at the lower value locations tend to be relatively concentrated. The degree of concentration generally increases toward the periphery as it does at the other centers. However, eating places (5812), optometrists (8099) and furniture stores (5712) are more dispersed than the other low value functions.

Relative Variability in Land Values

Comparisons of the variability in values between individual functions is not meaningful unless reference is made to the size of the mean about which variation occurs. The coefficient of variation is normally used to take this into account. However, because insufficient data is available to calculate the necessary standard deviations the index of variability used here is simply based upon the absolute range in values. The resulting indices for individual functions at each of the five levels of center is shown in Table 43.

In both the Rest of the City and in the Workingmen's area, variability increases directly with order in the hierarchy. For instance, neighborhood functions show an increasing index of variability at community and regional level centers. Similarly, community level functions have increased indices at regional centers. This regularity is to be expected since numbers of establishments for any given functional type increases directly with order in the hierarchy.

It follows from this that higher order functions will be associated with lower indices of variability than lower order functions. An example will make this point clear. Clothing functions are divided into community

TABLE 43

VARIABILITY IN LAND VALUES BY FUNCTION[1]

S.I.C. Code		R	C	N	Major	Minor
				Center		
R	5231	1.00	.45	-[2]	.34	
N	5251	.43	1.17	-	1.55	-
C	5311	1.54	1.50		.35	
C	5331	2.18	.97	.71	1.33	-
C	5392	1.60	.70		1.03	-
N	5411	1.32	1.07	.74	1.14	
N	10	2.03	1.48	.25		.46
N	5422	2.09	2.00	.29	.53	-
N	5423	1.39		-	-	-
C	5431		-		-	-
C	5441	1.83	1.21	-	.99	.54
N	5462	.80	1.52	.84	1.31	.11
C	5499	.83	.95			-
C	5612	2.44	1.12	.19	1.20	1.35
C	5621	1.77	1.35	-	1.63	-
R	5631	1.39	.68		1.25	-
R	5632	.92		-	.90	
R	5633	1.33			-	
R	5634	.14	-		-	
R	5641	1.54	1.11		1.14	-
C	5651	1.60	.96		.93	1.63
R	5662	1.02	-		.88	.81
R	5663	1.50	-		.60	-
R	5664	.31				
C	5665	1.79	1.15		1.23	.51
R	5671	-	-		-	
R	5699	1.80	-			
C	5712	2.35	.91		1.29	.29
R	5713	1.07	.44		.71	
R	5714	1.57	.54		.74	-
R	5715	.66	-			
R	5719	1.06	.61		.16	
R	5722	1.43	.86		1.15	
C	5732	1.87	1.11	.36	-	.29
C	5733	3.42	.48		1.37	-

TABLE 43 - Continued

	S.I.C. Code			Center		
		R	C	N	Major	Minor
N	5812	3.47	1.53	1.65	1.97	2.52
N	5813	1.71	1.40	1.23	.54	1.88
N	5912	2.35	1.41	.22	1.91	1.27
C	5921	1.76	1.35	.83	-	.81
R	5942		-			
C	5943	.93	1.37		-	
R	5952	1.42	.02		-	
C	5971	2.65	1.32	-	1.39	1.27
C	5992	1.29	.71	-		
R	5993		-		.42	-
R	5996	1.79	.66			
C	5997	1.34	.51	.98	1.55	
R	5999	2.51	.75		1.01	
C	60	3.17	1.61	-	.59	.75
N	605	1.83	1.19	.60		.83
C	6159	1.33	.78	1.10	1.84	-
R	64	1.54	-			
N	65	1.41	.98	.61		.61
N	7211	2.10	1.45	.81	.44	.68
N	7215	1.63	1.34	.29		1.10
R	7221	2.10	-		-	
N	7231	1.78	1.28	.13	-	
N	7241	2.47	.76	.69	.06	1.19
N	7251	1.92	1.56	.81		.14
C	7631			.63		-
C	783	1.24	.93	-		.53
R	7949	1.21				
N+	801	1.05	1.24	.52	-	-
N+	8099	2.25	1.53	.48	1.95	-
	Vacant	2.57	1.27		1.78	.98

Notes: (1) The numbers represent an index of variability derived from:

$$\frac{\text{absolute range in value}}{\text{average value}}.$$

(2) - indicates no variability in value.

N+ typical of the neighborhood level and all higher levels in the hierarchy.

level and regional level types. When these occur at the regional centers, the lower level community types have larger indices of variability than the higher order regional types. Similar ratios obtain for the different level types within the other functional groups.

In certain cases this regularity does not apply. In the Rest of the City, five functions are associated with lower variability indices at higher order centers. These are: hardware (5231), and bakeries (5462), stationery stores (5943) and delicatessens (5499). These all show a decrease in relative variability at regional centers. Eating places (5812) decrease in variability at community centers.

At major and minor centers, the regularity is less clear, and a greater number of functions shows a smaller index of variability of higher level centers. These include: men's clothes (5612), family clothes (5651), eating places (5812), bars (5813), banks (60), dry cleaners (7211) and barber shops (7241).

Summary

When the range in land value is used as an approximation of threshold range, a complex picture of overlap in thresholds between functions is revealed. Assuming that functions are able to occupy sites at any point within their value range, many functions are able to compete for locations at various parts of the retail nucleations. Thus, the extent of zones of overlap envisaged in the more complex model above must be considered a gross oversimplification of the pattern, but one that is necessary in order to comprehend the real world situation.

Both absolute and relative variability in land values increase directly with order in the hierarchy. This is expected since more establishments of any given type are found at higher order centers. Variations in the market served enable greater degrees of product differentiation between establishments, an extension of the threshold range, and result in wider geographical dispersion within centers. Some functions are, however, notably more concentrated within any given level center, and although product differentiation must also exist for these, they presumably are able to compete for higher or lower value land as the case may be.

CONCLUSION

An attempt has been made in this work to show how the theory of tertiary activity can be applied to the study of the internal structure of nucleated business centers. When the basic premises of the theory are related to aspects of land value theory, a meaningful framework is developed which not only accounts for a logical ordering of functions between alternate centers, but which also permits an understanding of their spatial arrangement within centers. This is based on the premise that high threshold functions are at the same time high rent paying functions. In this way the theory of tertiary activity is shown to have wider applicability in the study of the urban business complex than is at present realized.

Although we feel that the empirical evidence presented lends general support to the hypotheses investigated, it has not been possible to statistically substantiate them convincingly. This would seem to be largely due to shortcomings in the data, especially the poverty of the S. I. C. classification, the overlap in land values that results from the lack of values for individual establishments, and the naive index of threshold used. Nevertheless, the evidence presented suggests that this is a fruitful approach to the study of the internal structure of retail nucleations and that more penetrating research should be undertaken to obtain more refined descriptions and explanation than has been possible here.

To this end, it is suggested that future research should be directed toward:

(1) Establishing more realistic classificatory systems whereby functions can be differentiated on the basis of quality, and the range, or "bundle", of goods offered. Such a system would permit more refined statements about differences between and within alternate business centers.

(2) A more refined study of the effects of income differences on the structure of the hierarchy of retail nucleations, and on the types and quality of stores present at different level centers. For instance, it is most probable that any given order of center can in fact be disaggregated into a number of varying sized parts comprising different types and quality stores which service alternate levels of demand in the urban market.

(3) Finding a simple and operational method by which thresholds can be measured for individual establishments. This will enable the concept to be used with greater practical applicability in the study of urban retailing problems.

(4) More detailed case studies of the relationships between land values and business structure, and especially of the general level of values at different order centers; of the changes in the value pattern between and within retail nucleations through time; and of the effects of invasion-succession cycles on the lag in values at retail nucleations.

(5) More detailed case studies of the arrangement of functions at individual retail nucleations; of the effects of functional association on this pattern; and to include the study of upper floor uses.

(6) The study of the relationship between shopping habits and the location of retail functions within nucleated centers.

(7) The study of the relationships between store size, location, and threshold values.

APPENDIX A

THE RELATIONSHIP BETWEEN COOK COUNTY ASSESSED VALUES AND OLCOTT'S "BLUE BOOK" VALUES IN THE CITY OF CHICAGO

Two sets of land value data are available in the City of Chicago; first, those given in Olcott's Blue Book and second, the values of un-improved land assessed by Cook County tax department. The former are generally accepted as a fairly accurate approximation of the market value of land in the city. The latter, obtained for tax purposes, represent a percentage of this market value at which the property is appraised.

There are, however, numerous problems associated with the use of either source of value data. Firstly, difficulties arise from the form in which values are presented. Olcott's values are plotted on small scale maps, and consequently are not easily transferred to large scale plans necessary for more detailed study. The peak value is given for establishments immediately adjacent to the major intersection, but away from this corner values are presented on a half, third, and quarter-block basis instead of by individual establishments. Although assessed values are more detailed in that they are identified with specific parcels of land (a parcel of land being land under single ownership), it often happens that several different establishments occupy the same land parcel. In both cases, it is difficult to associate a specific value with a particular establishment.

Secondly, some doubt exists as to the reliability of value data. Of the two sources, Olcott's are perhaps to be preferred since they are derived initially from an analysis of property sales and sales stamp records. This is supported by Olcott's intuitive notions concerning changes in the relative value of land in the various parts of the city. Assessed values, on the other hand, are determined more subjectively by an individual assessor; and since values are assessed primarily for the purpose of taxation, the need to balance city budgets may perhaps guide the assessor and result in inflated values.

Thirdly, there is the problem of the availability of data. Olcott's values are presented in book form which may be readily obtained from any library. Assessed values are, however, the prized possession of Cook County, and are not readily obtainable to the public. In view of these shortcomings, Olcott's values are preferred on the assumption that the relationship between values given for a fraction of a block and the individual establishments it contains is not too much in error.

Least square regression analysis and the product moment correlation coefficient were used to establish the relationship between the two sets of data, and to test for a correlation between the allocation of Olcott's values to individual establishments and the more precise assessed values. Both types of data were collected for a random sample of four nucleations in the city. Three levels of analysis were used: (1) values for peak lots only in the sample centers; (2) values allocated on a half block basis in the sample centers; and (3) a case study of an individual center (63rd and Halsted) in which values were allocated to individual lots.

The data corresponding to each analysis are presented in Table 44. Since peak values are usually disproportionately higher than those of adjacent sites, thereby, perhaps, resulting in a biased correlation, they were treated separately. On the average, assessed values tend to be higher than Olcott's. The mean for peak values being, for example, 27.4 and 24.5 dollars respectively. Fourteen peak value

TABLE 44

RELATIONSHIPS BETWEEN OLCOTT'S AND ASSESSED LAND VALUES

Regression Equation

I Peak lot values $\qquad$ $Y_c = 4.19 + 0.7417\ (X)$

II Half-block values $\qquad$ $Y_c = 1.04 + 0.9260\ (X)$

III Individual lot values $\qquad$ $Y_c = 3.19 + 0.8220\ (X)$

Correlations

	R	R^2	N
I	.96	.92*	14
II	.99	.98*	45
III	.96	.92*	42

*Significant at the five percent level.

Reliability

	S_{yx}
I	5.63
II	1.8
III	3.4

observations are significantly correlated, with a coefficient of determination of .92. The regression coefficient of .74 indicates the greater rate of change of the assessed values plotted on the X-axis.

On the basis of half-blocks, assessed values were averaged out for that portion of the block corresponding to Olcott's data. The 45 observations were highly correlated with a coefficient of determination of .98. The low standard error of estimate (1.8) indicating that on average Olcott's values can be estimated to within 180 dollars from assessed values.

The case study of 63rd and Halsted included 42 observations of individual lots. A highly significant correlation was again found, the coefficient of determination being .92. The reliability of estimate was, however, somewhat less at this level, indicated by the lower standard error of 3.4. The regression coefficient of .82 indicates the greater rate of change of the assessed values. The consistency of this in all three analyses indicates that assessed values tend to overestimate higher values and underestimate those at lower levels. This is to be expected since highly valued property can support higher taxes, while the converse argument is applicable to lower valued land. Thus, assessed values would appear to offer a closer approximation of rent-paying ability than Olcott's values.

In spite of this, the difficulty in obtaining assessed values for all centers included in the study precluded their use, and so Olcott's values are used in this work. Each individual establishment was allocated the value given for the fraction of the block in which it was situated. Hence, values overlap a great deal, and the results of empirical investigation are not as refined as they would be if actual establishment values were available. Although the values associated with each establishment cannot therefore be viewed as an exact statement of the market value of the land, they are used in view of the fact that they are the most easily obtainable source of data.

APPENDIX B

THE DELIMITATION OF RETAIL NUCLEATIONS

Competition between alternative uses for sites within retail nucleations results in a decline in land values with increasing distance away from the maximum value at the peak intersection. At some distance away from the peak, values level off to form the generally uniform ridges of value associated with ribbon developments. The decline in values is not necessarily symmetrical about the peak intersection nor is it usually uniform on both sides of any of the intersecting streets.

In the zone where land values approximate those of the ribbon developments, nucleated functions give way to those typical of ribbon developments. Thus the boundary of any nucleation can be considered to be located somewhere in this zone of value transition. The problem of delimitation is, therefore, to find as accurately as possible where this point lies. This can best be done from the analysis of land value profiles.

Value profiles, the graphical representation of the decline in land values away from the peak, were constructed accordingly for each of the sixty-two nucleations in the study area. A typical profile is shown in Figure 29. This figure shows the decline in land values along the major streets intersecting to form the retail nucleation at 63rd and Cottage Grove. Two cross sections are illustrated; one through the intersection along 63rd Street, and the other through the intersection along Cottage Grove. The decline in land values is also shown for

189

190

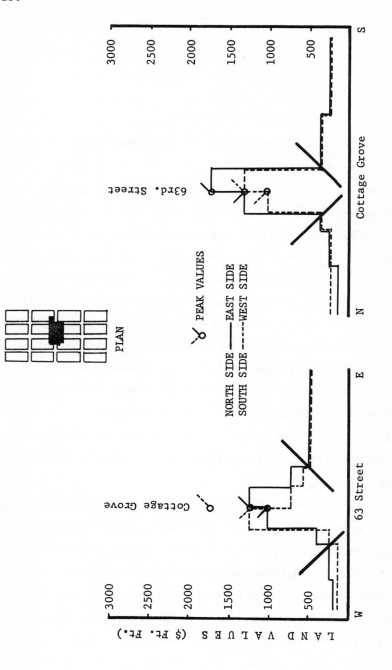

FIGURE 29: LAND VALUE PROFILES AT 63rd. AND COTTAGE GROVE

both sides of these streets.

There is a marked decline in values within a short distance from the peak values, which are seen to stand high above the levels of the adjacent sites. However, the rate of decline is not the same along both streets nor on both sides of the same street. There is a general symmetry, however, and the fairly smooth level associated with the ribbon developments is clearly distinguished. The curves are, moreover, noticeably stepped rather than smooth in form. This is attributed to the nature of the Olcott's value data, which it is remembered, were allocated on a fractional-block basis rather than by individual establishments. However, even if value data were obtainable on an individual site basis, the curve would still be stepped because of the areal extent of each property, but it would be characterized by less marked steps than in the profile illustrated in the figure.

The zone of transition between nucleated and ribbon functions is identified on each profile at the point where the curve levels off to form the ridge of value associated with the ribbon. These points at 63rd and Cottage Grove are shown on the cross section and on the plan view of the delimited center. Field investigation indicates that these coincide for the most part with natural breaks within the nucleation, such as alleys or other street intersections. They are undoubtedly the best approximations of the zone of change between nucleated and ribbon functions. In those cases where the natural breaks were not so readily observable on the ground or on the profile, field investigation was necessary to determine boundaries. Using the method, differences in the extent of retail nucleations along different sides of the street can be determined.

APPENDIX C

TYPES OF RETAIL AND SERVICE BUSINESS
With their Standard Industrial Classification and Frequency of Occurrence
in Retail Nucleations in the City of Chicago, 1962

S.I.C. Code		Frequency	S.I.C. Code		Frequency
5211	Lumber yards	1	* 5422	Meat markets	35
5221	Heating and plumbing dealers	8	* 5423	Fish (sea food) markets	9
* 5231	Paint, glass and wallpaper stores	22	* 5431	Fruit stores and vegetable markets	10
* 5241	Electrical supply stores	1	* 5441	Candy, nut and confectionery stores	45
* 5251	Hardware stores	33	5451	Dairy products stores	1
5252	Farm equipment dealers	1	* 5462	Retail bakeries, manufacturing	44
* 5311	Department stores	31	5491	Egg and poultry dealers	5
* 5322	Mail order houses, general merchandise	5	* 5499	Food stores not elsewhere classified, including delicatessens	19
* 5331	Limited price variety stores	51	5511	Motor vehicle dealers (new and used cars)	2
* 5392	Dry goods and general merchandise including "Army and Navy" stores	23	5521	Motor vehicle dealers (used cars only)	3
* 5411	Grocery stores, with or without fresh meat	39	5531	Tire, battery, and accessory dealers	14
* 10'	Supermarkets	43	5541	Gasoline service stations	13

APPENDIX C - Continued

S.I.C. Code		Frequency
5599	Miscellaneous aircraft, marine, and automobile dealers	1
* 5612	Men's and boys' clothing stores	50
* 5613	Men's and boys' furnishing stores	2
* 5621	Women's ready-to-wear stores	53
* 5631	Millinery stores	21
* 5632	Corset and lingerie stores	18
* 5633	Hosiery stores	12
* 5634	Apparel accessory and other specialty stores	13
* 5641	Children's & infants' wear stores	28
* 5651	Family clothing stores	21
* 5662	Men's shoe stores	28
* 5663	Women's shoe stores	27
* 5664	Children's and juveniles' shoe stores	5
* 5665	Family shoe stores	49
5671	Custom tailors	14
* 5681	Furriers and fur shops	6

S.I.C. Code		Frequency
* 5699	Miscellaneous apparel and accessory stores	7
* 5712	Furniture stores	49
* 5713	Floor covering stores	17
* 5714	Drapery, curtain, and upholstery stores	22
* 5715	China, glassware and metalware stores	4
* 5719	Miscellaneous home furnishing stores	16
* 5722	Household appliance stores	24
* 5732	Radio and television stores	38
* 5733	Music stores	33
* 5812	Eating places	62
* 5813	Drinking places (alcoholic beverages)	58
* 5912	Drug stores and proprietary stores	61
* 5921	Liquor stores	48
5932	Antique stores	5
5933	Secondhand clothing and shoe stores	4
5934	Secondhand furniture stores	3

APPENDIX C - Continued

5936 Secondhand automotive
      tire, battery and
      accessory dealers   1

5939 Secondhand stores
      not elsewhere
      classified   9

* 5942 Book stores   6

* 5943 Stationery stores   17

* 5952 Sporting goods
        stores   20

5962 Hay, grain, and feed
      stores   1

5969 Farm and garden supply
      stores not elsewhere
      classified   1

* 5971 Jewelry stores   49

* 5992 Florists   28

* 5993 Cigar stores and stands   21

* 5996 Camera and photographic
        supply stores   16

* 5997 Gift, novelty, and
        souvenir shops   42

5998 Optical goods stores   3

* 5999 Miscellaneous retail stores
        not elsewhere classified   35

* 601 Banks   41

* 605 Establishments performing
       functions closely related
       to banking   49

* 6159 Loans   35

* 64   Insurance agents, brokers,
       and service   17

* 65   Real estate operators
       (except developers) and
       lessors   42

701 Hotels, tourist courts
     and motels   2

* 7211 Dry cleaners   53

7212 Hand laundries   9

* 7215 Self-service laundries   35

* 7221 Photographic studies,
        including commercial
        photography   18

* 7231 Beauty shops   51

* 7241 Barber shops   58

* 7251 Shoe repair shops, shoe
        shine parlors and hat
        cleaning shops   33

7261 Funeral service
      crematories   15

7299 Miscellaneous personal
      service   5

APPENDIX C - Continued

S.I.C. Code		Frequency
733	Duplicating, addressing, blue-printing, photo-copying, mailing list & stenographic services	10
734	Services to dwellings and other buildings	3
735	News syndicates	4
736	Private employment agencies	5
739	Business services not elsewhere classified	9
7538	General automobile repair shops	4
7621	Electrical repair shops	5
* 7631	Watch, clock and jewelry repair	7
7641	Reupholstery and furniture repair	3
7695	Locksmith and gunsmith shops	4
7699	Repair shops and related sercices not elsewhere classified	1
* 783	Motion picture theaters	37
7911	Dance halls, studios and schools	2
7931	Bowling, billiards, and pool rooms	17

S.I.C. Code		Frequency
7949	Sports promoters, commercial operators, amusement and recreation services not elsewhere classified (includes motor clubs)	16
* 801	Offices of physicians and surgeons	30
* 802	Offices of dentists and dental surgeons	11
* 803	Offices of osteopathic physicians	1
* 804	Offices of chiropractors	1
* 807	Medical and dental laboratories	2
* 8099	Optometrists	44
811	Legal services	8
8231	Libraries	9
8641	Fraternal associations	1
8651	Political organizations	5
8661	Religious organizations including storefront churches	4
8662	Churches	4
891	Engineering and architectural services	1
8931	Accounting, auditing and bookkeeping services	3
899	Services not elsewhere classified	1

Notes : * Central functions
10' University of Chicago code

APPENDIX D

TESTING THE VALIDITY OF USING A RANKING OF FUNCTIONS
BY THEIR FREQUENCY OF OCCURRENCE AT CENTERS
IN THE STUDY AREA
AS A VIABLE APPROXIMATION OF A RANKING OF FUNCTIONS
BY THRESHOLD SIZE

Two investigations were undertaken to determine whether the ranking of functions by their frequency of occurrence at retail nucleations,
(henceforth called the frequency ranking), in the study area can be used
as a valid approximation of their ranking by threshold size. Firstly,
the frequency ranking for a sample of functions was compared to their
ranking by absolute numbers of establishments in the Chicago Standard
Metropolitan Area (S. M. A.). Secondly, the frequency ranking was compared to the ranking of functions by absolute threshold values derived
by Berry for Snohomish County, Washington, and Binford for Grant
County, Wisconsin.[1] In all three cases, significant rank correlations
were obtained and the frequency ranking was considered as a viable
approximation of rank order along the threshold continuum.

The first investigation was undertaken to see if there was any significant difference in the rank order of functions when the number of
centers at which they occur was used instead of total number of establishments. It was shown above that a direct relationship exists between
thresholds and numbers of establishments in an area. A ranking by
numbers of establishments is therefore similar to a ranking of functions
by absolute thresholds. However, because certain functions appear
highly centralized in a limited number of nucleations, a ranking by

frequency of occurrence at centers was considered more meaningful.

The number of establishments for a selection of functions in the Chicago S. M. A. is available in the Census of Business.[2] These are ranked in order of increasing ubiquity in Table 45, together with their frequency ranking. Spearman rank correlation was used to test the research hypothesis that the two sets of counts did not significantly differ. The calculated rank correlations was .85, which is highly significant at the one percent level. The research hypothesis was accepted and the ranking of functions based on their frequency of occurrence at centers is considered to be an accurate approximation of their ranking along the threshold continuum.

Using the frequency ranking as a viable approximation of the threshold continuum, a second investigation was undertaken to verify its similarity to the ranking of functions by empirically derived thresholds for Snohomish and Grant Counties. In both cases, significant rank correlations of .6 were obtained, and the frequency ranking was considered to be a viable approximation of the ranking of functions by threshold.

Because of the difference in functional classification used in this work and the others, it was not possible to compare the rank order of all 64 functions included in the Chicago analysis. Only a small proportion of this total could be used; 19 and 20 functions were selected from the Snohomish County and Grant County studies respectively. The functions included are presented in Table 46.

Marked differences in rank order are observed for certain functions. On the one hand, some low threshold functions in both of the rural areas appear to be relatively high threshold functions in the City of Chicago. On the other hand, the converse is true and certain functions which appear high threshold functions in the rural area studies occur as low threshold functions in the Chicago area.

TABLE 45

THE RANKING OF FUNCTIONS BY NUMBER OF ESTABLISHMENTS
IN THE CHICAGO S. M. A. AND FREQUENCY OF OCCURRENCE AT
CENTERS IN THE STUDY AREA

S.I.C.[1] Code	Areas		Ranking	
	(2)	(3)	(2)	(3)
5923	62	4	1	1.5
5715	91	4	2.5	1.5
5311	91	31	2.5	13
5942	141	6	4	3
5996	165	16	5	6
5713	225	17	6	7
5392	233	23	7	11
5719	237	15	8	5
5714	246	22	9	10
5993	262	21	10	9
5952	277	20	11	8
5431	304	10	12	4
5733	338	33	13	14
5732	431	38	14	15
5331	570	51	15	25
5997	603	42	16	18
5992	643	28	17	12
5971	666	49	18	23
5441	797	45	19	20
5462	973	44	20	19
5712	976	49	21	23
5665	1011	49	22	23
5612	1069	54	23	27
5422	1138	35	24	15
5921	1844	48	25	21
5912	1982	61	26	29
5621	1993	53	27	26
5813	6000	58	28	28
5411	6811	39	29	17
5812	7283	62	30	30

Notes: (1) A list of the functions identified by the S.I.C. Code is contained in
Appendix C.

(2) Number of establishments in the Chicago S. M. A.

(3) Number of centers at which each function occurs in the study area.

Source: U.S. Census: 1958 Census of Business - Retail Trade, Illinois,
Table 103, 1958 S. M. A. Establishments, Sales, Payroll, Personnel
and Kinds of Business, pp. 13-26.

TABLE 46

RANKING OF SELECT FUNCTIONS IN SNOHOMISH COUNTY (WASHINGTON),
GRANT COUNTY (WISCONSIN), AND THE CHICAGO STUDY AREA

S.I.C.[2]	Ranking[1]		
Code	Snohomish	Grant	Chicago Study Area
5812	1	2	1
5813	2	1	3
5722	3	5	16
7231	4	7	7
5251	5	3	12.5
5912	6	10	2
7241	7	6	4
5712	8	8	9
5331	9	11	6
5651	10	4	17
60	11	9	11
5992	12	17	15
7211	13	18	5
5971	14	12	8
7251	15	13	12.5
5952	16	20	18
5311	17	15	14
8099	18	14	10
5996	19	16	19
5462	--	19	12

Notes: (1) Functions are ranked in order of increasing threshold.

(2) See Appendix C for description of S.I.C. Code.

Rank Correlations.

A. Between Snohomish County and Chicago:

$$R_s = .6 \quad (R_s \propto .01 = .534)$$

B. Between Grant County and Chicago:

$$R_s = .6 \quad (R_s \propto .01 = .534)$$

These disparities are considered by the writer to reflect a fundamental change in the provision of certain goods and services which accompanies the increased density of population and different way of life in the urban area. The former is reflected in the closer spacing of centers and greater mobility of consumers in the urban area; the latter is the greater variety of goods and services offered at each level in the hierarchy and in the differences in tastes, needs, and preferences which accompany urbanism as a way of life.

For instance, household appliances and hardware stores are considered as high threshold functions in the Chicago study, but as low threshold functions in both of the rural area studies. This change in rank is expected since the role of these functions as independent suppliers of goods in the urban business complex is greatly reduced by competition from alternate sources.

A variety of appliance goods is offered from department stores, large furniture combines and discount houses; whilst a wide range of hardware goods is provided from drug stores, variety stores and supermarkets. The result of this is presumably reflected in the changing character of these stores in the urban area. It is conceivable that this change takes the form of increased specialization in order to satisfy the higher thresholds necessary from increased competition.

Conversely, dry cleaners rank high in threshold in both rural areas but low in frequency in the City of Chicago. They are typical town level functions in rural area central place systems. Below this level in the hierarchy, dry cleaners appear in a different form. Instead of individual dry cleaning establishments, the service is provided by one of the other business types as an adjunct of its main line. They constitute collecting agencies for a dry cleaner located in the nearest town. When thresholds are calculated from population:establishments ratios as they are in both of the rural area studies, dry cleaners are found to rank high in threshold.

Although it is expected that the increased population density of the urban area will be reflected in the increased number of dry cleaning establishments, it is felt that this is only part of the explanation for their low threshold rank. The demand for dry cleaning is notably greater in urban areas. City dwellers use dry cleaners more frequently than do rural inhabitants because of the different values attached to the presentation of self in the urban environment. Thus, a greater number of establishments of this type can be supported by a given number of people in the urban area than in the rural setting, and they consequently become low threshold functions.

A similar argument can be extended to the high rank order of bakeries in Grant County, (bakeries are not included in the Snohomish study), if it can be assumed that per capita demand for baked goods is less in rural areas. Given a higher per capita expenditure on baked goods in the urban areas, a greater number of establishments can be supported over and above the increase expected from the sheer changes in density of population.

It would appear that functions of certain types change in threshold as size of area from which they are supplied increases. If this is true, then it would appear erroneous to calculate thresholds from an overall population : establishments ratio in which all levels in the hierarchy are combined. Rather, it would seem more valid to calculate thresholds for each function at each level in the hierarchy separately. Future work should be directed toward establishing as exactly as possible what changes occur in the demand for various goods as level in the hierarchy increases, and to establishing the adaptations of business activities to cater to such changes.

[1] B. J. L. Berry and W. L. Garrison, "Functional Bases ....," op. cit., and L. Binford, "Thresholds for Functions in Grant County, Wisconsin," (unpublished Master's seminar paper, Department of Geography, Northwestern University, Evanston, 1961).

(2) United States Bureau of Census, Census of Business, 1958; Retail Trade, Illinois, pp. 13-26.

BIBLIOGRAPHY

Books

Berry, B. J. L. and Pred, A. Central Place Studies: A Bibliography of Theory and Applications. (Regional Science Research Institute, Bibliography Series, No. 1) Philadelphia: Regional Science Research Institute, 1961.

Chamberlin, E. A. The Theory of Monopolistic Competition. Cambridge: Harvard University Press, 1933.

Christaller, W. Die zentralen Orte in Suddeutschland. Jena: Gustav Fischer, 1933.

Dunn, E. The Location of Agricultural Production. Gainesville: University of Florida Press, 1954.

Garrison, W. L., et al. Studies of Highway Development and Geographic Change. Seattle: University of Washington Press, 1959.

Hoover, E. M. Location Theory and the Shoe and Leather Industries. Cambridge: Harvard University Press, 1937.

Hoyt, H. One Hundred Years of Land Values in Chicago. Chicago: University of Chicago Press, 1934.

Hurd, R. M. Principles of City Land Values. New York: The Record and Guide, 1905.

Isard, W. Location and Space Economy. New York: Wiley and Sons, Inc., 1956.

Kelley, E. J. Shopping Centers. Saugatuck: Eno Foundation for Highway Traffic Control, 1956.

Losch, A. The Economics of Location. Translated by H. Woglom and W. F. Stolper. New Haven: Yale University Press, 1954.

Olcott, G. C. Olcott's Land Values Blue Book of Chicago and Suburbs. Chicago: G. C. Olcott Co., 1961.

Ratcliff, R. U. Urban Land Economics. New York: McGraw Hill Book Co., 1949.

Rolph, Inez K. Nucleation: The Pattern of Retail Marketing. Chapter XIX of The Metropolitan Community. Edited by R. D. Mackenzie. New York: McGraw Hill Book Co., 1930.

Articles

Berry, B. J. L. and Garrison, W. L. "Recent Developments in Central Place Theory," Papers and Proceedings of the Regional Science Association, 4 (1958), pp. 107-120.

_____. "The Functional Bases of the Central Place Hierarchy, Economic Geography, 34 (1958), pp. 145-154.

_____. "A Note on Central Place Theory and the Range of a Good," Economic Geography, 34 (1958), pp. 304-311.

Berry, B. J. L. "Ribbon Developments in the Urban Business Pattern," Annals of the Association of American Geographers, 49 (1959), pp. 145-159.

_____. "The Impact of Expanding Metropolitan Communities upon the Central Place Hierarchy," Annals of the Association of American Geographers, 50 (1960), pp. 112-116.

Brush, J. E. "The Hierarchy of Central Places in Southwestern Wisconsin," Geographical Review, 43 (1953), pp. 380-402.

Carol, H. "The Hierarchy of Central Functions within the City," Annals of the Association of American Geographers, 50 (1960), pp. 419-438.

Getis, A. "The Determination of the Location of Retail Activities with the Use of Map Transformations," Economic Geography, 39 (1963), pp. 14-22.

Haig, R. M. "Toward an Understanding of the Metropolis," Quarterly Journal of Economics, 40 (1926), pp. 179-208 and 402-434.

Herbert, D. T. "An Approach to the Study of the Town as a Central Place," Sociological Review, 9 (1961), pp. 273-292.

Holton, R. H. "Price Discrimination at Retail: The Supermarket Case," Journal of Industrial Economics, 6 (1957), pp. 13-32.

Mayer, H. M. "Patterns and Recent Trends in Chicago's Outlying Business Centers," Journal of Land and Public Utility Economics, 18 (1942), pp. 4-16.

Murphy, R. E. and Vance, J. E. "Internal Structure of the C.B.D.," Economic Geography, 31 (1955), pp. 21-46.

_____. "Delimiting the C.B.D.," Economic Geography, 30 (1954), pp. 197-200.

Pred, A. "Business Thoroughfares as Expressions of Urban Negro Culture," Economic Geography, 39 (1963), pp. 217-233.

Proudfoot, M. J. "The Outlying Business Centers of Chicago," Journal of Land and Public Utility Economics, 13 (1937), pp. 57-70.

_____. "City Retail Structure," Economic Geography, 13 (1937), pp. 425-428.

Wendt, P. F. "Theory of Urban Land Values," Land Economics, 33 (1957), pp. 228-240.

Reports

Berry, B. J. L. and Mayer, K. M. Comparative Studies of Central Place Systems. A report prepared for the U. S. Navy, Office of Naval Research (Project NONR 2121-18; NR 389-126), Department of Geography, University of Chicago, 1962.

_____, et al. Commercial Structure and Commercial Blight. Chicago: Community Renewal Program, City of Chicago, 1963.

Cannoyer, Helen G. Selecting a Store Location. (U.S. Department of Commerce, Economic Series No. 56), Washington: Government Printing Office, 1946.

Proudfoot, M. J. Intra-City Business Census Statistics for Philadelphia. (U.S. Department of Commerce), Washington: Government Printing Office, 1937.

Ratcliff, R. U. The Problem of Retail Site Selection. (Michigan Business Studies, Volume IX, No. 1 (1909), pp. 1-93), School of Business Administration, Bureau of Business Research, University of Michigan, Ann Arbor, 1909.

Taylor, G. K. Relationships Between Land Value and Land Use in a Central Business District. J. C. Nichols Foundation Research Study, Washington: Urban Land Institute, 1955.

Unpublished Material

Berry, B. J. L. "Shopping Centers in the Geography of Urban Areas," Unpublished Ph. D. dissertation, Department of Geography, University of Washington, 1958.

_____, and Lillibridge, R. M. "Guides to the Provision of Shopping and Allied Service Districts in Residential Communities," Community Renewal Program, Chicago, 1962. (Mimeographed)

Getis, A. "A Theoretical and Empirical Inquiry into the Spatial Structure of Retail Activities," Unpublished Ph. D. dissertation, University of Washington, 1961.

Garner, B. J. "Land Values as a Basis for the Analysis of Functional Differentiation within the Central Business District." (Mimeographed)

Garrison, W. L. "The Business Structure of the Customer Tributary Area of the Fountain Square Major Outlying Business Center of Evanston, Illinois: A Study of the Dispersion and Agglomeration of Satellite Business Structures in a Portion of the Chicago Metropolitan Area." Unpublished Ph. D. dissertation, Department of Geography, Northwestern University, 1950.

Nystuen, J. D. "Geographical Analysis of Customer Movements and Retail Business Locations: 1) Theories, 2) Empirical Patterns in Cedar Rapids, Iowa, 3) A Simulation Model of Movement." Unpublished Ph. D. dissertation, Department of Geography, University of Washington 1959.

Proudfoot, M. J. "The Major Outlying Business Centers of Chicago." Unpublished Ph. D. dissertation, Department of Geography, University of Chicago, 1936.

Ratcliff, R. U. "An Examination into Some Characteristics of Out-lying Retail Nucleations in the City of Detroit." Unpublished Ph. D. dissertation, University of Michigan, 1935.